PEARSON

At Pearson, we believe in learning – all kinds of learning for all kinds of people. Whether it's at home, in the classroom or in the workplace, learning is the key to improving our life chances.

That's why we're working with leading authors to bring you the latest thinking and the best practices, so you can get better at the things that are important to you. You can learn on the page or on the move, and with content that's always crafted to help you understand quickly and apply what you've learned.

If you want to upgrade your personal skills or accelerate your career, become a more effective leader or more powerful communicator, discover new opportunities or simply find more inspiration, we can help you make progress in your work and life.

Pearson is the world's leading learning company. Our portfolio includes the Financial Times, Penguin, Dorling Kindersley, and our educational business, Pearson International.

Every day our work helps learning flourish, and wherever learning flourishes, so do people.

To learn more please visit us at: **www.pearson.com/uk**

How to Decide

What to do when you don't know what to do

JONATHAN HERRING

Harlow, England • London • New York • Boston • San Francisco • Toronto • Sydney • Auckland • Singapore • Hong Kong
Tokyo • Seoul • Taipei • New Delhi • Cape Town • São Paulo • Mexico City • Madrid • Amsterdam • Munich • Paris • Milan

PEARSON EDUCATION LIMITED
Edinburgh Gate
Harlow CM20 2JE
Tel: +44 (0)1279 623623
Fax: +44 (0)1279 431059
Website: www.pearsoned.co.uk

First published in Great Britain in 2012

© Jonathan Herring 2012

The right of Jonathan Herring to be identified as author of this work has been asserted by him in accordance with the Copyright, Designs and Patents Act 1988.

Pearson Education is not responsible for the content of third-party internet sites.

ISBN: 978-0-273-77039-8

British Library Cataloguing-in-Publication Data
A catalogue record for this book is available from the British Library

Library of Congress Cataloging-in-Publication Data
Herring, Jonathan.
  How to decide : what to do when you don't know what to do / Jonathan Herring.
    p. cm.
  ISBN 978-0-273-77039-8 (pbk.)
  1. Decision making. I. Title.
  BF448.H47 2012
  153.8'3--dc23
                                    2012004341

10 9 8 7 6 5 4 3 2 1
16 15 14 13 12

Cartoons by Bill Piggins
Typeset in 10/13pt ITC Giovanni Book by 30
Printed and bound in Great Britain by Henry Ling Ltd., at the Dorset Press, Dorchester, Dorset

Contents

Introduction

It's half-past two in the morning. You've got something on your mind and you haven't been able to get to sleep. You can't stop thinking about what you should do. You just can't decide. One moment you think you should say 'yes', but then two minutes later 'no' seems a much better idea. The more you think about it the more muddled you are. None of the alternatives feels right. You daren't make the wrong decision, but you don't know what the right decision is. Panic sets in and before you know it it's four in the morning and you are still trying to get to sleep. Indecision can be misery.

We've all been there. The inability to make a decision can be paralysing; the embarrassment of making the wrong decision can be awful. How on earth did we end up here, we ask? How could I have been so foolish?

Many people so dread making decisions that they simply do nothing – some have called it decidophobia! Please don't suffer from that; doing nothing is no way to get anywhere. Instead, make the decision to make decisions. Take control of your life.

One of the great things about being a grown-up is that you can make decisions for yourself. You don't have to follow the rules of parents or teachers: you can decide how to live your own life. You can lie in bed all day and stay awake all night. It can be Pot Noodles for every meal and you don't have to make your bed! There is FREEDOM! But with freedom comes the power to make choices, and for many people those decisions can be extremely difficult.

It is amazing what people will do to avoid having to make a decision, often at great expense: flipping a coin; looking at horoscopes; reading tea leaves; contacting a medium ... these can all be nothing more than a way of avoiding responsibility for making a decision. Why let tea leaves make a decision for you when you can make a perfectly good decision for yourself?

Reading this book won't mean that you will never again make a bad decision, but it *will* dramatically increase your chances of making a good decision. Quite simply, it gives you all the help you need to work through whatever decision it is you are facing, and reach that decision feeling happy that you've thought it through properly and you can now act.

This book will give you the confidence to make decisions, rather than avoid them. Dithering becomes a thing of the past. Anxiety subsides. Armed with the knowledge of how to go about making a decision, you'll feel calmer and more clear-headed, ready and able to face whatever decision comes along next. Read on!

Chapter

Preparing to make the decision

Before doing anything else, you need to make sure you're fully prepared to make the decision. This may sound like overkill, but in fact so many wise decisions fall at this basic hurdle. There are three key aspects to preparation. First, you need to define the decision to be made: know exactly what it is you are trying to decide. Second, you need to gather any and all relevant information. Third, you need to determine your priorities: what are you trying to achieve as a result of the decision? How are these priorities going to be ordered? Which are the most important and which are the least important? Without first taking these crucial steps it will be impossible to make a decision, much less a wise one.

What is the decision to be made?

This is often not a problem: you are quite clear what the decision is that needs to be made, you just need to figure out what to do. For example, you have been invited by a friend to go on holiday with them – do you go or not? Pretty straightforward, isn't it? But sometimes it's not that clear what the decision should be; you may feel unhappy with the situation you are in but you're not certain what the problem is. You can't decide what to do because you are not even sure what the question is. If you're clear on what decision you are making, then move on to the next section. But for those of you who find simply defining the decision difficult, here we go.

Many people spend a lot of time worrying or thinking about something but get nowhere because they are not focused on a particular question or issue. The problem 'I feel unfulfilled in my life, what can I do?' is impossible to address. You will be overwhelmed with the vastness of the question. Similarly, trying to decide 'Where shall I go on my summer holidays?' can lead to paralysis. With big questions or issues you need to focus on particular concerns which will help you identify the real question.

One way to do this is to break down big questions into little ones. So, rather than asking, 'How can I be happier?' ask, for example, 'Is there a hobby I'd like to pursue? I see there is a pottery class running on Tuesday evenings, which I have always fancied, would going to that class make me happier?' Or, 'What kind of holiday do I want: city or beach? What is my budget?' Break down the bigger, overwhelming question into smaller parts.

"Break down the bigger, overwhelming question into smaller parts."

If you are trying to decide whether or not to take a new job, consider a series of smaller questions: Will this job give me more money? Will the people I work with be nicer than the current ones? Will the commute be easier? Etc. Considering a whole set of smaller questions, which are more manageable, will start you on the way to making the bigger decision.

So by figuring out exactly what the decision is you are making, and whether it is possible to break it down into smaller decisions, you are defining the key decision(s) to be made. This is the first step of preparation! You might find it helpful to write down the exact decision (and sub-decisions) to be made – it is better than everything swirling about in your head. Take a piece of paper and write your decision question(s) down.

Shall I hire another person for the team?
Full time or part time?

What grade? More senior or less senior than Marie?

What will I do about Marie's position as a result?

Gathering the relevant information

Before making a decision you need to understand your current situation. This might sound like a no-brainer, but it isn't. Unless you know where you are now you cannot assess the wisdom of any change. So the first fact to establish is how you define your present position.

> "Unless you know where you are now you cannot assess the wisdom of any change."

To make this assessment properly you must be honest. In all areas of life it is easy to have a false impression of the truth. Some people see the best in everything and exaggerate how well they are doing; others see the worst and believe that everything is awful. I am sure we all know people who think they are extraordinarily beautiful when that's not exactly true. And there are others who are convinced no one could find them beautiful, when again that's equally far from true. So, too, in business it is easy to imagine your company is moving from success to success when a hard look at the figures would suggest otherwise. Rather than seeing the glass half-full or half-empty, it is best to see the glass precisely as it is. Know your current situation!

Gathering the facts you need to make a decision is an essential part of the decision-making process, but you must be careful: nothing is more dangerous than making assumptions about people or things. Particularly if they are the wrong assumptions! Let's start with looking at some good ways of finding evidence.

Good ways

Here are a few key tips:

- Rely on facts not feelings.
- Don't place too much weight on other people's views. Make your own assessment.
- Ask yourself where you were last year and also two years ago, this might help put your current position in perspective.
- Reliable sources. Sometimes you need hard facts. You need to know the distance from place A to place B. You need to know on what date your friend is getting married. You need to know when it is warm in Tenerife. If in doubt, double-check facts sourced from the internet by cross-referencing websites. Use reliable internet resources, such as university or government sites, or sites backed by a professional body.
- Seek professional opinions. Information on the internet tends to deal in generalities and common knowledge. Sometimes only a professional can give you the exact information you need. This is especially important in areas such as law and accountancy, where the cost of errors can be substantial. Seek the opinion of an expert, too, when necessary. For example, if you need specific advice on a legal issue, you may find the general legal principles on the internet, but for advice on how they apply to your case you may need to speak to a lawyer in a specific relevant field of law.
- Be aware of the temptation to present the facts in the way you want the decision to go. Try to be objective. Don't reject a fact because it doesn't fit in with your current thinking. If you want your business to renew a contract it is tempting to emphasise the evidence supporting things which are going well with it. To make a good decision you need to be objective.

Making a decision based on false or incomplete facts will go wrong. It is like baking a cake without all the ingredients. So, always get as many facts together as possible to support your decision making.

Some people love information, statistics and opinions. When buying a new kettle they will spend many a happy hour poring over internet sites to work out the benefits of different kettles and their attributes. Others avoid the facts and go with instinct – if the first kettle they find on the internet looks OK, then that's fine, they go for it.

You will not be surprised to know that, generally speaking, information lovers tend to make better decisions, because they have more facts to base their decisions on. I am sure we have all experienced buying something on the internet in a hurry only to discover when it arrives that it was not quite what we were expecting. We should have taken all the necessary time to gather all the relevant information before we pressed that button.

But it is not always that easy. There is a cost to finding information. Maybe the three hours looking at kettles on the internet saved you £2, but was your time worth that? There are tiny differences in the features of kettles which can be uncovered with extensive research, but will they be worth the hours of time and the ensuing headache? Make sure that the time you spend on researching facts for the decision is in proportion to the usefulness of the information you are gathering.

Bear in mind, too, that too much information can simply overwhelm you to the stage where making a decision becomes impossible. Having to compare the details of fifty kettles is probably more than most people can deal with. There is some sense, therefore, in restricting your search to a limited number of trusted sources. For example, 'I will only look at kettles of this brand,' or 'I will only look at these three websites to see what offers they have'. Similarly, if you are in business and are making a decision involving just a tiny sum of money it may be more efficient to make the decision quickly and spend the time saved researching information for a bigger decision.

"Too much information can simply overwhelm you to the stage where making a decision becomes impossible."

Where do you want to be?

You will never get where you want to be unless you know where you are going! With a SatNav you put in the postcode of your destination to enable the device to work out the best route; so too in decision making it is key that you work out where you want to be. In your ideal world, where would you be? What are your goals?

Don't think your goal has to be something grand. It might be something as straightforward as wanting to have a good time. If you know exactly what your goal is you can skip to the next section. If you know what you want but you don't know how to get there, read on.

It is easy to be afraid of the question 'What are my goals?' because you think you will never get there: you might wish for an enormous house and a fast car, but you don't want to say that because you can never imagine you will have them! However, to make good decisions you need to face up to what your end goal is. Maybe what you assume you want your end goal to be is not actually what you really want it to be! Perhaps with more thought your ultimate dream will not be a big house and a fast car, but a house in a neighbourhood surrounded by good friends and good public transport links.

So be prepared to dream, but think carefully whether the dream is really what you want. It may be that when it comes to it you can't get your dream, but you can take steps towards it and get as close as you can. Unless you know what you want, what you really, really want (thank you, Spice Girls!) you will not get there. A personal aside: I really wanted to be a solicitor. I did a law degree and began practising in London. It was my dream, and what I thought would make me happy. But I hated practising law. The reality wasn't as pleasant as the dream. I went back to university to do graduate work, and now I teach law. I am as happy as I could imagine. So sometimes what we dream of at first is not necessarily the best choice for us, but we only realise that when we get there.

Some people will find this part easy, other people will not. You might not be sure what your goals are. Maybe you think you have no goals. Well, in that case, ask other questions:

- What do I enjoy doing?
- What am I good at?
- What makes me comfortable?
- Who else do I know whose life I admire?

Answering these kinds of questions might help you define what interests you have and where you might like to be.

Once you have determined your goal, never lose sight of it. A common error in decision making is to be so side-tracked by all the alternatives and arguments for and against that you lose sight of what you are really trying to achieve. If at the end of the day your decision has not taken you towards your goal, something has gone wrong. If you go out shopping for a new pair of shoes and come back with no shoes, but yet another jumper, something has gone wrong. Sadly, for too many people that happens and they end up asking: 'How on earth did I end up *here*, when I was trying to get *there*?' You can waste a huge amount of time and money by losing focus on your ultimate goal. We recently decided to fix up our kitchen. That was our goal. However, the architect presented us with plans to have a new dining room, merge the existing kitchen and utility room into a new, larger kitchen, and make the playroom into a new utility room. Sound confusing? It was also twice as expensive! So we looked at what we were trying to achieve – fixing up a 30-year-old kitchen – and we kept that as our primary goal.

"Once you have determined your goal, never lose sight of it."

If you have a big decision to make now, spend time on this question: where (in an ideal world) would you like to be in relation to the decision? Write that goal down in big letters and keep focused on it. Even if you do not reach it now, you can start taking steps to reach it by making smaller decisions along the way.

> My goal is to increase output by 10%.
> We need more orders, but our sales staff are overstretched.
> Shall I hire another person for the team?
> Full time or part time?
> What grade? More senior or less senior than Marie?
> What to do about Marie's position as a result?

Prioritise your goals

It may be that in thinking about the issues you are facing there are a variety of goals you have: to make some closer friendships; to spend more time with your children; to have time to enjoy your hobbies. You need to think carefully about how you prioritise your goals. First of all, you will need to rank them: which is the most important? If you could only achieve one of these, which will it be? Then (and this is the stage that is often forgotten) you need to try to think about how important each of your goals are. Give them a mark out of ten. Perhaps you will rank them as follows:

- More time to enjoy hobbies: 9
- More time with the children: 8
- More time with friends: 6

Or:

- More time with hobbies: 9
- More time with children: 4
- More time with friends: 3

In the latter case you have decided that spending more time enjoying your hobbies is much more important than your other goals – which you would like to achieve, but which are far less a priority than your hobbies. In the first case, your hobbies and children are very closely ranked, so it might be better to look at which is more achievable from a practical point of view.

You might wonder why ranking is so important. We will discuss this more later, but notice that if you find a solution to your decision which does not allow you to spend time with hobbies but does allow you to spend more time with children and friends, the first ranking is fulfilled but the second isn't. Depending on your ranking, that solution might or might not be the one for you.

What needs to change to get to your goal?

List all the things you can think of that are barriers to you reaching your goal. The kind of things you might consider will depend on the type of decision you are making.

In a business context you will be looking at figures: if you are making a loss, what will need to change to move your company into profit? It may be that there are several things that could be changed: cutting costs; increasing prices; expanding customer base; etc. At this point you are not deciding what needs to be done, but simply what different things could change to reach where you want to get to.

You need to be very careful at this stage. It is very easy to imagine barriers which are not there and to see as barriers things that are not. Here are some common dangers:

- **Don't assume that other people are the problem**. It is so easy to see other people as the problem and not you yourself. 'If only my colleague was not so obnoxious my work life would be happy.' 'If only my partner stopped complaining our relationship would be good.' You have to be brutally honest here: are you winding up your colleague? Is your partner complaining for good reason?

- **Don't assume you are the problem**! The opposite is true for other people: they assume that all their problems are their fault. 'I keep saying the wrong things to my colleagues and making them annoyed.' 'I keep forgetting to do what my partner has told me and annoying him.' Again you need to be honest: are your colleagues simply short-tempered? Is your spouse being unreasonable?

- **Don't make the 'if only' mistake**. It is easy to assume that there is only one barrier to our goals. I am sure we have all done this: 'If only I could move house I would be happier,' 'If only I could pay off that debt everything would be better.' By fixating on what appears to be the 'big barrier' you can lose sight of the goal or how you can get there. The truth is that normally there are a range of barriers and what you think will solve your problems will not. Moving house will not make you happier if what is in fact causing unhappiness is your lack of friends.

- **Who you are and what you do are not the same thing!** Many people are unhappy with aspects of their personalities or their lives and believe that by altering one thing they will change the kind of person they are. Beware of thinking you will be transformed from being a bad-tempered, selfish and argumentative so-and-so into a loving person just by changing your job or relationship. It's just possible that might happen, but many people think they can transform themselves just by changing their circumstances, and that doesn't often happen. If all your colleagues are impossible to work with but when you change jobs your new colleagues are just as difficult, it may be that you are the problem, not them!

Conclusion: Keep your focus

I realise that there has been a lot to think about in this chapter. You may even have found it overwhelming, but don't give up. Keep focused on the key things you need to know at this stage:

- What decision am I making?
- Do I have all the facts, including an understanding of my current position?
- What are my goals?

It is so easy to get distracted by the 'But what about this?' and, 'Have you thought about that?' questions that you can lose sight of the central issue you are meant to be thinking about.

Chapter

2

What drives decisions – and what should drive them

You want to make excellent decisions; the problem is that it's easy to be influenced without realising it. You need to be aware of the natural tendencies that we all have which can take our decision making off course. Equally, there are factors that *should* influence your decision making that you can easily ignore. It is important to think about this right at the start.

What should not drive decisions

So what are the things that might drive our decisions, but shouldn't?

Fear or lack of fear

One of the things that many people find hardest to deal with is risk. This keeps a lot of people from making decisions. We should acknowledge that for many people an irrational bias can take over when it comes to risks. Consider these two people:

- AMY: If I go outside I might be hit by lightning and so it is safest to stay inside.
- BRINDA: I am so good at driving that even if I drive at 100mph I can drive safely.

Amy has placed far too much weight on the risk of being hit by lightning. So much so that it is ruining her life. Quite literally, she needs to get out more! Indeed, tragically, she may be putting herself more at risk by staying inside (and not getting exercise or having friends) than by going out.

Brinda, on the other hand, has greatly overestimated his driving ability when speeding. He is endangering his life and the lives of others because he is confident that the statistics don't apply to him. This is a common problem, when individuals think they are outside the law and perfectly safe in what they are doing, and is a selfish and inconsiderate way to approach life.

Look back on your life and think about whether you are the kind of person who is always terrified of risk or is happy-go-lucky. You don't need to change, but do try to be aware of your natural inclination and make sure it does not lead you to make irrational decisions. If you are naturally cautious that's fine, but make sure you are not being absurdly so. Similarly, if you are naturally a risk-taker, that's not a problem, but be careful that you keep risks to a reasonable level.

"Think about whether you are the kind of person who is always terrified of risk or is happy-go-lucky."

When considering statistics in relation to risk it is important to keep a clear head. Here are some key points in understanding statistics:

- Virtually everything has a risk; we wouldn't get out of bed in the morning if we were trying to avoid all risk of harm. In fact, come to think of it, we wouldn't stay in bed either – what if the ceiling fell in? So just because you can see a possible bad consequence for a decision does not mean you should not do it. Everything has a risk.

- Assess the risk. How likely is it to happen? Imagine doing the thing 100 times – how often would the bad result occur? Amy should imagine going outside the house 100 times; how often would there be a lightning strike? Zero. That means it is a negligible risk. However, if you drive at 100mph how likely is it that there will be an accident or you will get caught by the police? 50 times out of 100? Maybe more. It is therefore a much higher risk.

  So many people make the mistake of making a decision on the basis of hoping to avoid a (dubious) disaster, rather than because it will move them towards something wonderful. Don't miss out on the best for fear of the worst.

- Consider not just the likelihood, but also how bad the thing you are risking is. It may be worth taking a fairly high risk of a small harm. Travelling on public transport carries a risk of catching a cold in winter. Most people think the risk is worth it if it is easier going to work on public transport and getting a cold is perceived as not too bad. However, it is high risks of disasters that you want to avoid at all costs. If your house is burning down, it is best not to go in to get anything!

- Are the risks inevitable or can you reduce them? Driving a car carries a risk; this can be reduced by wearing a seat-belt and driving carefully. You also should have insurance, which will cover the risk of an accident should one occur. If you are worried about booking a holiday because you might fall ill, travel insurance won't reduce that risk but it will help you in the event that it does happen. If you are think-ing of embarking on a new relationship and are worried it will not work out, perhaps you should make sure you have a network of friends who will support you if it goes wrong. In any situation ask yourself, do you have an alternative? If things go wrong, do you have alternatives that are nearly as good? And is there any way you can reduce your risk?

Acknowledge the pressures

Sometimes we feel under pressure from others about a decision. Your girlfriend very much wants to get married and she will be very upset if you say no. Your business partner is very keen to pursue a venture and will be disappointed if you do not agree. You have been offered a job and you know your parents will be thrilled if you accept.

It is, in fact, almost impossible to make a decision without feeling under pressure from somewhere or someone. The key point is that this is *your* decision. You will have to live with the consequences of the decision, not your parents or friends. Never make a decision just on the basis that you are doing what someone else wants you to do – it's not a good reason to do it. So be aware of the expectations and hopes of others, and take them into account, but make sure you do not skew your decision making just to please them. Remember you are the one who is making the decision and you will be responsible for it.

"Remember you are the one who is making the decision and you will be responsible for it."

Other people may disagree with your decision and may be disappointed in you, but having gone through the processes in this book you will be able to justify your decision. You are not being wilful or selfish or petulant; you have thought through the issues available and used sensible decision-making techniques to arrive at the best result.

Are you in the right mood?

In 450 BC Herodotus made the following statement:

> 'If an important decision is to be made [the Persians] discuss the question when they are drunk and the following day the master of the house ... submits their decision for reconsideration when they are sober. If they still approve it, it is adopted; if not, it is abandoned. Conversely, any decision they make when they are sober is reconsidered afterwards when they are drunk.'

I'm not sure I would recommend that approach but it shows that decisions can only be made if we are ready to make them. Sometimes we are in an emergency and a decision has to be made – there is no time to lose – so at the end of this book there is a chapter on making decisions in a hurry. However, in other instances, if the decision is important it needs to be made with care and you will need time and a calm mind to make it.

Above all do not make a decision when you are angry. An angry decision is likely to be one caught up in the moment. It is unlikely to be thought through. I am sure we have all said or done things in anger that we deeply regret. Good decision-making needs a cool head, not a hot one.

"Do not make a decision when you are angry."

Similarly, make sure you are in a steady mood. It is easy to make a rash decision when you are feeling very happy, which is why some firms try to sell property to people on holiday. They know holidaymakers are having a good time and are excited about being in a new place and so they will probably have their guards down. Be wary about making a major decision when you are deliriously happy, for you are looking at the world through very tinted spectacles!

The same is true if you are feeling down. When everything is grey and you can see only gloom you will not be able to assess the reality of your situation. You need a realistic look on the world if you are to make a good decision. If possible, wait until you are feeling more equitable.

That said, avoiding decision making is a disaster. Too often people are waiting for things to change but are not making a decision about how to change things. Usually change just does not happen. If things are not as you would like them to be you need to make a decision to change them. Beware of thinking that you will 'wait and see' – there may be some occasions in which that is sensible, but too often that is an excuse not to recognise there is a problem. It is a way of avoiding making a decision about what to do.

For many people worry is a real barrier to making a decision. It might even stop them thinking about the decision they are to make. Don't worry – you can do something about this. A problem faced is better than one that eats away at you. Don't worry, but take action. Although you may be nervous about making decisions, in this book you will find the tools to make an excellent decision. Taking it step by step will help you to make a decision that is logical and justified.

Remember this, too: for many decisions there is no one right answer. What outfit to wear or whether to buy new shoes can cause worry and sometimes terror ('what will people think?'), but your decision is unlikely to result in a disaster. Or perhaps you choose to go on holiday to Greece and have a great time.

You would probably have had a great time if you went to Italy instead. There is not necessarily a right answer to lots of everyday decisions, and once we recognise that, the agony can be taken out of decision making.

What should influence you?

Decisions are not just based on facts, although those are important, they are also about values – what matters to you. This is why I can't make decisions for you, nor you for me – we're each unique in how we see the world around us. We all have different beliefs and we all want different things out of life.

And that's important when it comes to making decisions. The kind of person you are, the values that underpin your life, and your core beliefs will, and should, influence what decisions you make.

A common error in decision-making is for a person to make a decision while forgetting their values. They are later riven with guilt because they made a decision they are embarrassed about or which they later decide was morally wrong. You don't want to do that. So, although I'm sure you're eager to get on to the 'how to make the actual decision' part, it's well worth taking a minute to remind yourself of what matters to you.

Values

Values are the things that are most important to you – the rules you live your life by; your moral guideposts. I can't tell you what your moral values should be, that's a matter for you, but you need to be clear about what yours are. For most people these turn on two key questions:

1. **What are your absolute moral principles?** Most people have certain things that they would never do, or would never do unless there was an exceptionally good reason for it. Virtuous people will insist we should never lie, not even 'white lies', while others believe that lies are justified if they

achieve a greater good. You might think there is a difference between lying to a friend and lying to a business client. You might believe that promises must never be broken or that adultery is always wrong.

If you have moral principles of this kind, be clear about what you believe. Apply your principles to the decision you are trying to make. Do any of your moral principles come into play here?

If you do have a strong moral principle, stick to it. Moral principles are only of value if you hold fast to them when there are persuasive reasons not to. If you are only honest when someone is looking, you cannot really claim to be honest. If you are only faithful to your partner when there is no strong temptation not to be, you cannot really claim to be faithful.

It may be that you're not sure what the moral thing to do is. In that case you can't go far wrong by using the principle 'treat others as you would like to be treated yourself'.

2. **What are your goals? What are you looking for in life?**

You need to view the decision against the backdrop of both your values and where you are heading in life. If you are trying to decide whether or not to cancel a dull commitment so you can go on a fun day out instead, you need to know if you are ultimately seeking instant gratification or a virtuous character. If you're trying to decide whether to leave your job and retrain in another role you need to think about whether your driving value in this situation is more money or a deeper sense of job satisfaction. If you're not sure, think about which of the options has made you more happy in the past – when you've felt most content and fulfilled – or what you'd like to be remembered for. You might love watching DVDs, but in the end will you look back with pride at the fact that you watched over 10,000 DVDs during your life?

So your values will include these absolute moral principles and also what you are looking for in life. Some people may feel a bit uncomfortable with all this talk of morals and values, but these don't have to be anything high-minded. You may decide that the key value for you in a particular decision is making money. That is, of course, common. Most people when purchasing something will be seeking to get value for money, and most people when making business decisions are seeking the deal that will achieve the most profit.

It might help to have a look at these words below: which four would you most like to have associated with your life, and how might that desire affect the decision you need to make?

Abstinence	Excitement	Justice
Adventurousness	Fairness	Leadership
Altruism	Faith	Love
Belonging	Family	Making a difference
Boldness	Fidelity	Obedience
Calmness	Fitness	Openness
Carefulness	Fun	Originality
Cheerfulness	Generosity	Patriotism
Commitment	Goodness	Professionalism
Compassion	Grace	Prudence
Contentment	Happiness	Restraint
Control	Hard work	Selflessness
Correctness	Health	Self-reliance
Courtesy	Honesty	Sensitivity
Creativity	Honour	Serenity
Dependability	Independence	Strength
Determination	Ingenuity	Success
Effectiveness	Insightfulness	Thoroughness
Elegance	Intelligence	Uniqueness
Empathy	Irreverence	Unity
Enthusiasm	Joy	

When thinking about your values you might want to distinguish between your central values and your fun values. Most of us have things we enjoy doing – watching a particular TV series, cooking on a BBQ – but these are not what 'make us us'. They do not represent defining characteristics. Not many people when asked 'What kind of person are you?' would say, 'I am a TV watcher'! Fun values are different from our central values: these might be religious, an ethical code, a political belief, or support for a football team! Central values would be how you define yourself: what you see as an integral principle for you. Thinking through this might help you decide whether things you enjoy are actually central to your identity or are in fact rather more superficial values – while these may still be important, they are less so than the central values. Knowing your central values can certainly aid you in the decision-making process.

One final point: remember your values may change during your life. You may once have been religious but now have lost your faith, or you may have found a new faith. In younger days having fun may have been a priority, but now establishing family life is paramount. This does not mean that the values you had at the time were wrong, it is just that for some people values change. Certainly don't assume that the values you once had are necessarily the ones you still hold dear. That said, those who have strong moral values will often hold them throughout their lives.

"Don't assume that the values you once had are necessarily the ones you still hold dear."

Be self-aware

As part of being self-aware, let's explore some of the common differences people will bring to their decision making:

- Risk-averse; risk-takers. We have already seen on p.18 that there are those who avoid risks like the plague and those who seem to revel in risk, who are confident that bad things will never happen to them. Which are you?

- Do you rely on thoughts or feelings? There are those who focus on rational thought and have no regard for emotions or gut feelings. There are others who much prefer dealing with matters by instinct. Most people use a combination of rational judgement and intuition, but are likely to have a preference for one or the other.

- Do you prioritise yourself, your family or your community? Some people make decisions based on what is best for them, others place much more weight on the interests of others. Are you the kind of person who typically thinks about others and is willing to help others, even if it is inconvenient to you? Altruism is, if you like, the opposite of selfishness. Altruism puts others first, whereas selfishness puts the self first. Of course, few people are purely altruistic, and few people are purely selfish – most people are somewhere between the two. But where you are can affect how you weigh up the different factors when making decisions. The more altruistic you are, or wish to be, the more weight you will place on the interests of other people. But be careful: considering only others and not yourself could end up meaning you become so miserable you are no help to anyone. You must look after yourself and protect your health and well-being, even if that does sometimes mean other people must come second.

- Do you seek perfection or is 'good enough' sufficient? Are you determined to achieve the ideal in what you do or are you happy if things are good enough for the job? Depending on your outlook, your decisions will certainly reflect this characteristic. Your opinion can make group decisions more difficult, as some people are happy for a good enough result while others require the perfect solution.

- Do you find you are often complaining, or do you hate grumbling? Some people are highly conflict-adverse; they hate the idea of upsetting someone or having to complain about something. They will pay the restaurant bill even if the food was awful. They will say nothing to the employee who is always phoning in sick, rather than put in disciplinary proceedings. However, by contrast some people are much more forthright and do not shy away from any kind of confrontation or disagreement.

- Do you tend to prefer the familiar or the new? Many people have a preference for the familiar, which is why they go to the same place on holiday each year. If it is very important to you that you do not make a mistake, choosing the familiar may be sensible. If you are organising your mother's 80th birthday you may prefer a venue you are familiar with over one you are not. Conversely, some people always prefer something new and relish exploring unknown terrain. Knowing which personality you are will guide your decision making.

- Are you a person who is influenced by appearance? This is a common divide among people. For some appearance is just frippery; who cares what someone is wearing when what matters is their character, their views, what they are like and what they do? To them spending time on appearance is a waste and highly irrelevant – they just grab the nearest shirt and jeans and move on to the important business of life. This trait normally extends to other areas, too. Why worry whether the car is clean or dirty as long as it goes? The cover and appearance of the report is irrelevant, it is the content that is key.

  For others appearance is crucial: they believe that you need to look decent to be taken seriously. If you cannot take the time to make your appearance smart you are reflecting a slovenly, lazy attitude to life. If your report is not easy on the eye and is untidy, to them that suggests the thinking in it is untidy too. To people who value appearance, smartness and neatness is an outward mark of an inner reality.

  The difficulty is that both sides can have a dim view of the other. To the 'anti-appearance' brigade the 'pro-appearance' lobby appear fixated on the trivial; while the pro-appearance brigade see the anti-appearance lobby to be untidy and inconsiderate.

In listing these factors I do not suggest that one side is good or the other bad, but that you should make sure you know yourself. Do you tend to be selfless and put little weight on your own interests? If so, be careful in your decision making that you are not downplaying your own interests too much.

Do you tend to seek perfection? Have you ignored a good-enough option that might be the best? If you know your own biases you don't need to change them, but at least be aware of how they have influenced your decision and so be willing to explain why you decided the way you did.

Know your needs

It may help when thinking about personal decisions to consider carefully your different needs. Here is one way of thinking about them:

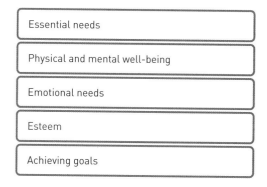

Essential needs

Physical and mental well-being

Emotional needs

Esteem

Achieving goals

Your basic needs are your essential biological needs: what you need to live. Water, food, health care and so forth. These are the most important needs you have. Unless the situation is completely dire you should never make a decision which leaves you without these.

Next there are safety needs: you must protect your physical and mental well-being. Without a healthy emotional and physical life you will not be able to help others or function well in society. People who are very altruistic and put the interests of others way above their own interests risk endangering their own well-being to such an extent they are no help to others and in fact become a burden. As with basic needs, unless you are facing a desperate situation do not make a decision which risks causing you serious mental or physical harm.

The next thing to think about are emotional needs: having a sense of belonging, a place within society, and of loving and being loved. These are central to a person's emotional well-being; they are important in making a person feel content.

Understanding your emotional needs leads naturally on to the next in the list, esteem: the need to feel valued both by others and oneself. Many studies have been done which show that having a good self-esteem helps in all parts of life, and in our case, decision making. Valuing yourself and your opinions, as well as feeling valued and listened to, is an important need that should not be disregarded.

Finally, self-actualisation looks at reaching the things that give you a sense of achievement and purpose. These needs include fulfilling your plans and feeling successful. Self-actualisation means realising your potential, and if unmet these needs can lead to much unhappiness. However, sometimes our sense of belonging and the commitments we have might mean we cannot satisfy all our plans. We can't meet all our self-actualisation needs. For example, our role as a parent might mean that we cannot pursue a particular business venture. Understanding our self-actualisation needs, and knowing when it is possible to meet them and when they have to be postponed, is a great help in decision making.

When making a decision that will affect your personal life you could consider how the decision will affect all these different needs that you have. It is also useful to rank your needs to see which are really integral to you.

Summary

After reading this chapter you should have a clearer sense of who you are and what matters to you. An understanding of these factors is crucial in making an excellent decision. Be aware of your tendencies and the pressures that you face – they might set you off on the wrong course. Don't be misled by your own preconceptions or pressures from others. Before embarking on the decision-making process, try to work out possible dangers:

- Do you tend to avoid risk at all costs or do you enjoy the thrill of risk-taking?
- Do you feel under pressure from others to make a decision in a particular way?
- Are you in the right mood to make a decision?

You will not necessarily be able to remove all these influences, but if you are aware of them you can make sure they do not have undue significance in your decision. Instead, be clear on what you hold dear. Make sure you act in line with your principles, values and goals. Then you can make a decision which is the right one for you.

Chapter

3

Choosing the tools to make the decision

To make a good decision you need something to structure your thinking. Something to help you lay out your options, weigh them up, and then select the best one. There are many models that do just this, and it doesn't matter too much which you opt for – all do the same basic job – but they differ in *how* they structure your thought process. Different people feel a natural affinity with different models, so choose the one that you feel most at home with, the one you can imagine using.

Five decision-making models

1. Pros and cons

This is perhaps the most familiar way of making decisions. Imagine you are to decide whether to pursue a particular course of action. List the arguments in favour (the pros) and list those against (the cons). It is best to give each pro or con a score out of ten, with ten points indicating a very strong point, down to one point if it is not particularly important. For example, let's say you are considering buying a new car. Your list might look like this:

PROS	CONS
The old car keeps breaking down: 8	A new car costs a lot of money: 9
The new car can carry more people: 5	Insurance may increase: 2
The new car is greener: 3	
TOTAL Pros: 16; Cons: 11	

Buy the car! The decision seems easy, but there is a caveat: even though there are more points in favour for buying the car, if you do not have the money and borrowing would put you in a very tenuous financial position, then don't buy it. Sometimes one single 'con' can outweigh all the 'pros' if that con is insurmountable. But by using the pros and cons approach what you have established is that you really do *want* the car, so it might be that you would be willing to take on a second job to pay for it. Outlining the relevant pros and cons is hugely beneficial in defining the elements that will affect your decision.

An adaption of this approach may be to add a third column headed 'Interesting' or 'Unknown', in which you should list factors which you are not sure are positive or negative. Or there may be issues that you know are controversial but on which you have a view. Identifying such issues is important if you are going to have to justify your decision in a work context, for example, or if you are making the decision on behalf of someone else. This will help clarify whether you are making the decision based on facts … (obvious pros or cons) or on personal preferences (subjective factors). Taking the example of buying a car, a third column could be:

"Clarify whether you are making the decision based on facts … or on personal preferences."

PROS	CONS	INTERESTING
The old car keeps breaking down: 8	A new car costs a lot of money: 9	Sentimental value of old car: 2
The new car can carry more people: 5	Insurance may increase: 2	Friends may feel jealous: 2
The new car is greener: 3		
TOTAL Pros: 16; Cons: 11; Interesting: 4		

Even if you combine the 'cons' and 'interesting' columns, still the argument would come down in favour of buying the car. Your 'pros' outweigh the negative and variable factors combined.

2. Grid analysis

Grid analysis can be particularly helpful when you are choosing between several options. It involves the creation of a grid in this form:

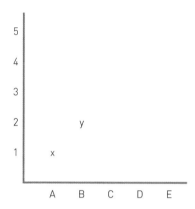

List the options you are considering (A–E) and list the key aims (1–5). Score out of ten each option you are considering against each aim. So in x you will put how option A scored against criterion 1, and in y how option B scored against factor 2. If some of the options are more important than others you could give a lower maximum score. For example, if aim 5 is less important than the others, mark it out of 5 and the others out of 10.

To determine which is the best option you simply add up the scores for each and see which is the highest.

In the example overleaf someone is considering what present to buy their boyfriend for his thirtieth birthday. They have listed the five possibilities at the bottom and the five factors on the left. The different factors are marked out of 10. The girlfriend wants to get him a present that will help him in his job, be unusual, will last a long time and is cheap. She realises that this may be impossible! But by using grid analysis her choice will become more clear:

	Hot air balloon ride	New suit	20 books	Course in public speaking with famous actor	iPad
Unusual	10	2	2	8	3
Good for job	0	8	3	10	1
He will enjoy	8	1	9	2	7
Long lasting	2	7	6	6	5
Cost	3	4	6	5	7
TOTAL	23	22	26	31	23

3. Force field analysis

In a way this is a variation on the pros and cons approach. You look at the forces that are supporting a decision and the forces that are pulling in the other direction. Think of a piece of putty which is being pulled. You might draw a diagram like this:

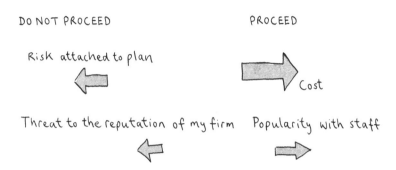

In this illustration the size of the arrows would indicate the strength of the 'pull' in each direction. One thing you can then do is consider whether there is a way of reducing or increasing the pulls. If there is a financial risk to the decision, can it be covered by insurance? Could you increase the popularity of the decision with staff by providing an incentive? By investigating ways of reducing or increasing the pulls you are seeking to discover where the pull is clearly in one direction.

4. Six thinking hats

Edward de Bono developed the 'Six Thinking Hats' model for decision making. Some people find it a helpful way of dealing with problems, although it does not work for everyone by any means. This method encourages you to think about issues from a range of perspectives and seeks to keep you from 'thinking in a rut'.

	You should focus on the facts. What facts do you have? How many more facts do you need?
	Put on your rose-coloured spectacles and be positive. Look everywhere you can for the benefits of the alternatives. If all goes really well, what will happen with the different choices?
	Look for the negatives. Play devil's advocate. What is the worst-case scenario? If it all goes horribly wrong, where will you be?
	Here the focus is on your gut feeling and intuition. What are your fears or likes, loves and hates? What is your heart telling you to do? How will others react emotionally to what you plan to do?
	Here the focus is on creativity. Forget the obvious answers you have thought of, is there a way of looking at this completely differently? Turn it on its head. What would a child say?
	This focuses on being rational.

The idea is to put on these different hats (metaphorically, of course) to look at the problem. This decision-making method is perhaps most effective for a group discussion. You can encourage everyone to talk about the issue with the same hat on. This will avoid the all-too-common problem of one person addressing the group in terms of emotional points and another with arguments about the facts of the matter, and the parties not really progressing the discussion at all. Rather than being at loggerheads, if everyone is, say, wearing their top hats and discussing the benefits from this particular point of view the discussion stays focused.

I personally see the Six Thinking Hats method as brilliant for thinking around the issues, but it doesn't make a final decision easy to reach, as there is no ranking of factors involved. It might be that in considering all the issues the answer becomes obvious and the ranking of factors is unnecessary. When making a decision, there is nothing better than thinking about it from many points of view and the Six Thinking Hats is a very good model for doing so.

5. Tree diagrams

For some people (at least in the UK) the word tree diagrams brings them out in a cold sweat. Their use in schools can put people off them for life, but they can be helpful in decision making, especially in thinking through the consequences of a decision. Start with your essential problem and draw lines with the options. Like this:

You then need to think through the questions that might arise as a result of your decision:

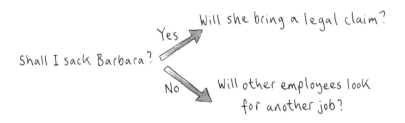

These made lead to further questions:

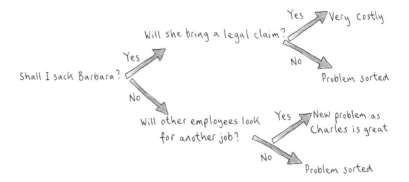

Of course, it is likely that in a case like this the tree diagram would be more complex and there would be more options to consider.

A tree diagram can be a helpful way of thinking through the possible consequences of taking a course of action. You might end up with many branches, depending on how far ahead you wish to think, but this method delineates action and consequences, cause and effect. Having used a tree diagram you will be better placed to make your decision on the original question.

Summary

You are well on your way to making a great decision. You now know what the question is that you are asking and are aware of the dangers you may face as you make the decision. You have selected your decision-making tool. Use the one described in this chapter which is best suited to how you feel and think; the one you can imagine you (or your group) can use effectively. Now it's time to decide.

Chapter

Making the decision

Well done! You are now ready to make the decision. You have thought carefully about the questions you need to ask, you have gathered the relevant information, you have foreseen some of the pressures you are under and the risks you may face and you have considered what your values are and what kind of person you would like to be. Finally, you have selected one of the decision-making tools we discussed in Chapter 3 and so now it is time to make your decision.

If you find you can, go ahead and make that decision.

If you find you can't, then you won't be alone. Many would-be decision makers are likely to have a problem choosing A or B. The most likely reason at this point is: you don't know how much weight to give a particular factor. You cannot decide if you think it is more important that your car is economical or whether it is trendy. Often two factors seem equally crucial. There are some particular issues which people find difficult to weigh and we will consider them here.

1. The opinions of others

How much do you care about the opinions of others? There are some people who are very concerned about the opinions of others: 'I love these jeans, but people will laugh at me'; 'I think this is the best decision but my staff will think I am going soft'; 'I would love to buy that car, but my friends will think it is extravagant'; 'I don't really need this new gadget, but everyone else seems to have one.' If you find yourself thinking like this, be careful. It is easy to fall into the trap of making the decisions you think others would expect you to make, or making the decisions that everyone else seems to be making. Those are not necessarily the right decisions.

If you feel concerned about what others will think, ask yourself some more questions.

1. What exactly is it that I am worried others will think?
2. Will they be justified in thinking that? Will their impression be correct?
3. Do I respect their judgement?
4. How will they react if I make a decision they don't agree with? Will I lose that friendship, or lose their respect?

If you believe that what people will think will be mistaken, then their views deserve little respect. If they think less of you because your jeans are not a trendy label, doesn't that say something bad about them, rather than about you? If their views are irrational or not based on the values that you hold dear, there is no need to pander to them. However, you may decide their views *do* carry validity. If you fear your friends will think you extravagant, they may be right. Think carefully whether that would be a fair criticism for them to make and then weigh that up against the other factors you need to take into account.

2. Emotions

Emotions are an important part of decision making. This can be demonstrated with the much-discussed case of a man known as Elliott. Elliott had undergone surgery to deal with a small tumour on his brain. Before the operation he had had a rewarding life: a happy family life; a successful job; and he was active in his community. However, the operation had changed Elliott's life. Although he had the same IQ (in the top 3 per cent of the population) he could not make decisions. It took him ages to make even the most obvious decisions: what television programme to watch; where to park the car. Because of this change in his behaviour Elliott lost his job and became divorced. His neurologist eventually identified the problem: Elliott was devoid of emotion. When shown photographs with a dramatic image – a severed foot, a house on fire – rather than responding with emotion as most people would, he appeared to feel nothing. Elliott was capable of thought, but did not feel anything. Without emotion, he could not make decisions. Elliott's sad story shows us that decision making is not, therefore, entirely a matter of thinking; it involves feeling, too.

Jonah Lehrer argues that our reliance on emotion comes down to evolution. The brain has had to learn to react instinctively. When chased by a mammoth there is no time for the rational brain to work out the correct response: emotion has to take over. Run! Impulse overrides the rational brain. We rely on cues and hints that are not rationally processed. Lehrer gives the example of a batsman hitting a ball in a cricket match. He estimates normally the batsman has about five milliseconds to decide how to hit the ball. That cannot, he suggests, be an entirely rational process. The instinctive reaction of the great sportspeople involves picking up on tiny clues on which they can respond intuitively.

If, therefore, you are having difficulty in placing a value on the different factors that you are taking into account in your decision, trust your instinct. Go with how you feel.

"Trust your instinct. Go with how you feel."

There is another important issue around emotions, that is that you should beware of making decisions in the face of bad news or misfortune. When faced with some calamity our instinct can be to believe 'well, it can't get worse'. You can see this in action in the TV show *Deal or No Deal*. As fans know, there are 26 briefcases of varying amounts from a tiny sum to a very large sum. The contestant does not know how much is in each case, but must choose one. This case is locked away. The contestant can then open the remaining briefcases one at a time. Each time, the contestant is made an offer by 'the banker' and can choose to keep that sum of money or carry on opening up briefcases in the hope he will either get a better offer from the banker or that the final (locked-away) case might contain a huge sum. Gradually, as more cases are opened, the contestant will get an idea of what his or her locked-away briefcase might contain. The game is at its most exciting when a contestant is left with, say, four cases (including the locked-away one): worth £1; £50,000; £100,000; £250,000. The contestant might then be offered £75,000 by the banker. This is a good offer if his locked-away case contains £1 or £50,000 but it is not a good offer if it contains one of the larger sums. So, in our case if the next case opened was £250,000, that would be a real disappointment as now the locked-away case could only include £1, £50,000 or £100,000. The banker in such a scenario typically makes a generous offer, say £65,000. In statistical terms that is a good offer to take. On average it is likely to be better, much better, than what is in the locked-away case. Yet contestants typically reject it. Researchers have noted that if contestants feel they have lost out on earlier decisions they will reject even reasonable 'offers' from the banker. Having lost out on the £400,000 their disappointment seems to skew their thinking. Like the addicted gambler, having lost once they sink their losses even further. The emotional reaction to bad luck can lead to bad decisions.

This is supported by an interesting experiment carried out by an economist, Richard Tharler. He asked people two questions. First:

> Imagine that you have decided to see a movie and have paid the admission price of $10 per ticket. As you enter the theater, you discover that you have lost the ticket. The seat was not marked, and the ticket cannot be recovered. Would you pay $10 for another ticket?

Of those questioned 46 per cent said they would buy another movie ticket. He then asked another question:

> Imagine that you have decided to see a movie where admission is $10 per ticket. As you enter the theater, you discover that you have lost a $10 bill. Would you still pay $10 for a ticket to the movie?

This time 88 per cent said they would still buy a movie ticket. Now in fact there is no real difference logically between these two scenarios. In both cases they were down $10; it is just that in the first case they have lost the $10 having already spent it, and in the second the loss of the money is just one of those things that happen. People's emotional reactions to the situation were subjective though the amount of loss was equal.

Despite this, you should always be careful about making decisions when you have received disappointing news. Beware of the gambler's instinct to believe bad luck could not hit you twice; be careful not to pour good money after bad. Feeling cheated or the victim of bad luck is not a good frame of mind in which to make excellent decisions.

"Beware of the gambler's instinct to believe bad luck could not hit you twice."

3. Don't make decisions based on personal comparisons

It is easy to place weight on a factor because you want to be better, or look better, than others. Avoid that temptation. Wherever you are in life you will find there are others who are better at something than yourself. If you are always seeking to be the best you will find you are invariably disappointed. You need simply to decide what is best for you. It does not matter if this is more or less; higher or lower than others. If it is right for you, that is all that matters.

In Dan Ariely's book *Predictably Irrational* he gives the example of this point in another context. It involves, of all things, breadmakers. Apparently when the first bread-making machine was put on the market it did not sell well. The company then introduced a new, more expensive model and the older model started selling well. It was not that people suddenly decided they wanted to make bread, but the original model now appeared to be a bargain as compared with the new model. People, it is said, think in relative terms rather than absolute terms. This is why people are tempted to buy a product on sale because of the appearance of a bargain, whereas they would not buy the same product at the same price if no mark down was indicated.

4. Make sure you are not prejudiced

We can often make judgements based on unknowns. Studies suggest that many prejudicial beliefs are based on ignorance. Racism is best countered by getting people of different races to get to know each other. People who have negative attitudes towards gay people often don't know any gay people. Don't make the mistake of assuming negative things about people or groups or plans just because you have never come across them before. Be open to new ideas; new ways of thinking about things; new people. Your assumptions might be reinforced; but they might as easily be challenged and you will have opened up a new way of looking at the world.

"Be open to new ideas; new ways of thinking about things; new people."

Summary

We have seen in this chapter some of the issues which people struggle with when operating the decision-making tools. If you've entered all your information into your decision-making model and are struggling to decide, remember:

- Listen to your emotions, but also be aware of how your emotions can impact on your decisions when experiencing misfortune.
- Don't hold prejudices: be open to new things.
- Think in terms of what will be of benefit to your goals. Don't put too much weight on comparison.
- Give due weight to the views of others, but not too much. It is your decision after all.

Chapter

5

Help! I still can't decide

Some people find decision making really difficult. It could be that even after all the advice I've given so far you still don't feel ready to decide. Let's look at why. First we will address why decisions are difficult, and next we will look at common pitfalls.

Why are decisions difficult to make?

There are several good reasons why a decision might prove especially difficult to make:

1. **The future is uncertain**. This is perhaps the most common reason why a decision will be seen as difficult to make. You do not know if the holiday in France will be fun or not. You do not know if there will prove to be a market for a particular product. You do not know if married life with your partner will be a success.

   If you are faced with a decision like this, the first thing you need to do is to accept that you are never going to know what the future holds for sure. All decisions have to be made on the basis of the best available evidence. If you think you cannot make a decision until you are sure what the future holds, then I am afraid you won't get up to much in your life. There will always be an element of risk attached to a decision as none of us knows what the future holds.

"Accept that you are never going to know what the future holds for sure."

Given, therefore, that the future cannot be known for sure, you have to make predictions about the future. I am not talking here, of course, of visiting a clairvoyant, rather you need to estimate the likelihood of something happening. What has happened when you did things like this before? Did you enjoy them? If so, you are likely to enjoy them again. Do people you know who generally like the same kind of holidays as you enjoy going to this place? Have businesses you admire taken a similar decision? You can learn by looking at examples of comparable decisions around you, and thereby gain an inkling of how it might work out for you.

There is always a temptation to choose the 'known' over the 'unknown'. If you have been to a restaurant you have enjoyed before you may choose to go there again rather than try a new restaurant. But don't get stuck in the mud, especially when the stakes are low. Unless it's a very important date, try somewhere different. It's unlikely the new restaurant is going to be a disaster. It might even be better than you thought!

2. **You don't know what you want**. You have two job offers: each has its benefits and disadvantages and you cannot decide between them. One has a better salary, but the other looks more fun. One has a shorter commute, but the other is a more prestigious company. One has the chance of bonus payments, the other has higher job security. You need to go back and make sure you are clear on your key values. What is most important for you in this new job? At the end of the day is money the most important criterion? Or is it the prestige of the job? Look through the different factors and try to rank them in order. Maybe you will come up with a list like this:

   1. Salary
   2. Job security
   3. Friendliness of colleagues
   4. Length of commute
   5. The possibility of bonus payments
   6. The prestige of the company.

You are now well on the way to ascertaining how to balance the pros and cons. But we are not quite finished yet. We need to rank these a little more precisely: give them a mark out of 10 to indicate how important they are to you. You may then produce a list like this:

1. Salary: 9
2. Job security: 8
3. Friendliness of colleagues: 4
4. Length of commute: 3
5. The possibility of bonus payments: 2
6. The prestige of the company: 1

If this is the list then we can see that for you salary and job security are the two key goals, and you should focus on those. The other matters only need to be considered if on the first two goals the jobs are equal.

However, imagine you had put this:

1. Salary: 9
2. Job security: $8\frac{1}{2}$
3. Friendliness of colleagues: 8
4. Length of commute: $7\frac{1}{2}$
5. The possibility of bonus payments: 2
6. The prestige of the company: 1

That would indicate that the first four factors are all pretty important to you. Indeed the job with the best salary may not be the best choice if the other job scores better in terms of security, friendliness and the commute. Knowing what exactly you want will help you make your decision when faced with more than one viable option.

3. **What is right and what is best**. This can be a genuine dilemma which can make a decision really difficult. The course of action which you think is most likely to achieve your goals infringes one of your moral values; the decision which will promote your well-being is spending Christmas with your girlfriend, but you feel you ought to spend it with

your parents. You are going to have to weigh up doing what is right and what will give you more pleasure.

Remember our discussion on values earlier. Do you want to be the kind of person who acts in a certain way? If you are really stuck, most people put a high value on being loving. If you ask: 'What would a loving person do in this situation?' you are not going to go far wrong.

The division between your values and what seems best can be particularly acute in the business setting. Here, the temptation to make the decision which will make the most money can be strong. But ask yourself what reputation you will gain as a result. A person who makes a dishonest decision may make a short-term gain, but he or she is likely to pay the price in the long term. A reputation for being unreliable or driving an absurdly hard bargain may bring you success for the deal on the table, but it is not going to lead to an ongoing mutually beneficial relationship. Remember, a reputation for being honest or reliable can be lost with a single lie or breach of a promise.

"A reputation for being honest or reliable can be lost with a single lie or breach of a promise."

Deciding between what is right and what is best often happens in family relationships. You know what is best for your children, but is it the morally right decision? You might be fervently against private education, but you feel the state system is not providing for your child's educational needs. Seeing the tension between your moral values and your child's needs helps delineate the decision. If you do have to compromise your values, at least you are making the conscious decision to do so.

The decision between values versus need also affects moral decisions. One current debate is in the use of embryos for stem-cell research. If you need treatment, and the only treatment available is using embryonically-derived stem cells (but you are morally against this), can you justify putting your values to the side?

Many decisions are not easy. Recognising that what is right is not always what is best, or vice versa, is key. Being stuck in the wasteland in between leads to indecisiveness. Understanding there is a dilemma is part of working out a decision.

4. **Unnecessary focus on the past**. Looking backwards is one of the biggest barriers to decision making. Something awful has happened and you have to decide what to do, but sadness or bitterness at what has happened is impeding your decision-making. Your partner has left you; you suddenly find you are in serious debt; your boss fires you. All of these solutions are likely to generate feelings of bitterness or perhaps blame: why did this happen to me? How could he behave so badly? How did I get into this position? These are important questions which you do need to think about. But you also need to look forward. Separate out dealing with the past and making decisions for the future. You need to keep a clear head and look forward, not back.

If you have been sacked, ask yourself how can I go about finding a new, even better, job? If you have been dumped, ask how can I find a new, better partner? Focusing on these questions and making decisions as to how to deal with them, is, in the long term, going to be more practical than dwelling on what has happened. We can always learn from past life experience, and that can inform our decision making, e.g. 'I won't make the same mistake again!', but unnecessary wallowing in the past can be a true hindrance. Be positive and proactive!

Common pitfalls

1. **You just can't quite decide**. If you have gone through the preparation for making a decision and have selected the method you would like to use to do so, there is no good reason for not making the decision. The systems discussed already have provided you with the logical way to proceed. If two options score the same, and all the factors balance out, then just choose one or the other. Flip a coin if all else is equal!

   If you realise you have problems with indecision it may help to set yourself a time limit. If someone has asked you to make a decision, try to give them a time by which the decision will be made. Say, 'I will decide by Wednesday if I will take the job,' and stick to the deadline.

2. **You don't decide**. Don't forget that not making a decision ends up with the decision being made for you. You see a job advert you might be interested in but can't decide whether to apply for it. Before you know it the deadline has passed. You see a flat you might be interested in renting, but before you get round to deciding to contact the estate agent it has been let. Spur yourself into making the decision. Take control of your future and don't let events just happen.

   Don't misunderstand me, it may be that having thought through all the issues you feel you don't know enough to make a choice, or that now is not the time to make the decision. That is perfectly reasonable. You have at least made a decision not to make a decision! Just don't let an issue pass you by through procrastination.

3. **Don't lose sight of the wood for the trees**. A common mistake to make is to lose sight of the key issues. This is particularly true if some of the decision-making tools we have just discussed are used in great detail. There may be ten factors in your 'no' column and only one in the 'yes' column, but the one 'yes' factor may be hugely more important than all the others. Keep focused on the primary goal. If you have decided to put in a new kitchen so that you have room for a new cooker, don't let a decision about spending all your money on granite worktops mean you end up with a kitchen without a new cooker.

4. **Don't overcomplicate!** One writer has produced this equation on whether you should ask someone out on a date:

$$\frac{W + G + 2A_Y}{3A_H} - \frac{R^2}{20} = A_{sk}$$

I won't bore you with what the letters stand for, but I think I for one would have spent so long struggling with the maths I would have forgotten what I was meant to be working out! Follow your heart and don't make things difficult for yourself. If you have got bogged down with one of the tools, try using the tool again but just with your top three factors. One of the problems with the tree diagram method is that you can have over a hundred branches! Stick to the issues which are paramount to your decision.

5. **Exaggerating fears**. I have already talked about this but it is important and so I will raise it again here. Some people become paralysed by fear and miss out on all kinds of interesting things because they are terrified of doing them. Other people seem willing to take absurd risks for a quick thrill. Most of us are not at the extremes but somewhere in between. Know what your predisposition is: do you tend to exaggerate risks or underplay them? Take that into account when making your decision: is this really a genuine risk or something fanciful? Calmly evaluate the risks involved in your decision.

"Know what your predisposition is: do you tend to exaggerate risks or underplay them?"

6. **Not being honest with yourself.** It is easy to stack up the data against making the right decision. You see what you want to see and don't see what you don't want. You listen to the people who agree with you and ignore those who don't. That's dangerous. Don't be nervous of facts which would point in a different direction or not listen to people who differ from you. Don't stop when you have found one piece of evidence in favour of your initial view. Find all the facts. Look at the facts. Listen to others' views and give them appropriate weight. Rarely are all facts pointing in one direction or will everyone agree. You can take contradictory evidence on board, even if in the end you do not follow it.

7. **Not being self-aware.** We all have our prejudices; they may be political views or religious ones. Know what your individual predispositions are. It may be we have colleagues that we do like and some that we don't. Beware of letting your in-built prejudices cloud too much the decision that must be made. Your best friend at work may be supportive of a decision, but try to be objective. Evidence may be produced by an organisation you don't like, but that does not mean the evidence does not carry any weight. Think rationally and be open-minded.

8. **Unreliable memories.** This is a common human trait. We remember the good things and forget the bad. Most people will look back on a holiday as a week of bliss or on a Christmas with family as a time of unalloyed joy. The reality may have been that in both cases while a lot of fun was had there were also times of difficulty. For many people human memories glamorise what has happened. That is no bad thing, but beware of this when you come to make decisions. Always looking at the past with rose-coloured spectacles will not aid you in learning from past decisions.

9. **Trying to make the 'perfect decision'**. It is easy to think that every problem has an ideal solution and that if you spend enough time thinking about it the answer will emerge. But for many decisions there is no right answer. Often you will be very happy with either option you are trying to choose between. People spend hours deciding on the correct menu for a dinner party or the right colour for the spare bedroom, but in truth you'll not notice whether the wall is white with a hint of apricot or white with a hint of peach in a few weeks' time! So don't get hung up on getting it right. Often you can't go wrong: make the decision quickly and spend the time you've saved doing something more interesting!

10. **Sometimes the decision must be made between bad and worst**. Sometimes life throws you a bad deal. We have to accept that is just the way it is. Don't avoid making a decision because it will produce harm; sometimes there is no option but to cause harm. Do I tell my friend her boyfriend is cheating on her or do I say nothing? Harm is going to result in that case whatever you do. In that scenario it is not your fault. Make the decision which will cause the least harm and do everything you can to lessen the harm. But don't avoid making a decision because it will hurt someone. Not doing something will hurt too. It's just a question of which will hurt more.

11. **Having low self-esteem**. Some people make bad decisions because they do not trust themselves. It is easy if you think you are foolish or not good enough to simply follow others. This is not a good idea. You need to recognise that you are an expert in yourself. You know your deepest longings and values. No one else does. You are entitled to make the decision which you judge right. Don't let others impose their will on you. Remember, you are the one who is going to have to live with the decision and therefore you are the one who is going to make it. You may need to be brave because you are making a decision others disagree with, but it is your decision and you have good reasons for making it, so act.

12. **The dangers of the 'slippery slope' argument**. The slippery slope argument often arises in decision making. It involves arguing that if you allow one thing, which seems reasonable, then a host of other less desirable consequences will follow. For example, if a parent allows their child to stay out one night, that will lead to the child staying out every night. A slippery slope argument can be a reasonable argument, but we need to be careful with it. A neighbour asks to park a car on your drive or in your parking space for an evening. Some people are tempted to reason like this: 'Where will this all end? Once I allow them to park for one evening, they will start doing it every day. And I will never be able to use the space.' Or, 'If I grant this pay rise, everyone will come into the office demanding a pay rise and the firm will go bust.' Now these 'slippery slope' arguments (if I allow X then I will have to allow Y, etc.) can keep one from being generous or fair because of the fear of your generosity being abused.

    Slippery slope arguments can be useful but they also need to be treated with great care in case they are given too much weight. First, think how likely it is that the dreaded scenario will arise. If your neighbour asks you for a pound to buy some milk, is it likely that if you give it to them they will be asking you for £5000 next? If that is probable, don't lend one pound! But it is highly unlikely. And wouldn't you want to think your neighbour would lend you a pound if you were stuck? Second, you must consider whether you can prevent the slippery slope arising. Is there a reason why one individual employee should receive a pay rise and not others: e.g. that there has been a change in their job description? Then even if you are inundated with requests you may be able to explain that there is a good reason just to give the one employee a pay rise.

13. **Keeping your options open**. When making decisions it is tempting to do everything we can to keep options open. While this can be valuable, it can also hide an unwillingness to make a decision. You don't buy the new computer you need because you think that a new model may appear soon

which will be even better than the current one. Is it realistic that next year's computers will be that much better than this year's? Is any improvement likely to be worth the inconvenience of waiting until next year? Or often people don't book a holiday for fear a friend might come up with a better idea. That might happen, but if not you may be left with no holiday. Keeping your options open is often decision avoidance in disguise. Be aware of this. Unless there are very good reasons for keeping options open, just decide!

"Keeping your options open is often decision avoidance in disguise."

14. **Attaching too much weight to the 'herd'**. Everyone else may be taking their business in a certain direction, but you don't need to follow them. If you have calculated that a different direction is better, stick to your decision. Particularly in the business world, the maxim 'it is in doing something different that success is often found', proves to be true. Following the crowd is easily presented as the safe option: 'Look at all of them, they can't all be wrong.' Well, they can be, as history attests. In 1637, tulips were being sold in the Netherlands for vast sums, ten times the annual wage of a skilled worker. It seemed sensible to those buying to purchase at this price because other people were doing the same thing, but soon the market collapsed and those who had been paying high prices for tulips just because other people were deeply regretted following the crowd.

15. **Don't be swayed by images**. Another danger comes from focusing too much on what you can see and experience. In a study, Paul Slovic, a psychologist, showed some people a picture of a starving child from Malawi and asked if they wished to donate to Save the Children. To another group of people he gave a list of statistics about starvation in Africa and asked for a donation. This group gave, on average, half the amount than the first group who saw pictures of a starving child. In many ways this is illogical. The information

about the many starving children should be more effective an argument for donating than seeing an image of a single child. The reasons are, no doubt, that the emotional reaction to the single face elicits a stronger pull than the intellectual disclosure of the facts.

Still can't decide

Let us imagine you have used the pros and cons method and you still cannot reach a decision. That might be for one of three main reasons:

1. The decision-making process has not led to a clear conclusion. The pros and cons are about equal.
2. The decision-making process has reached a clear conclusion but you feel unhappy with it.
3. You have reached a decision but are worried that more information may come to light.

Let's look at each of these cases separately.

It's all equal

Suppose you have used one of the decision-making models outlined in Chapter 3 and there is nothing to choose between the options. The pros and cons are equal. The sums from the grid lead to the same total for two options. Help, what do you do?

Well, the good news is that it looks like you have two equally good alternatives. You are spoiled for choice. No reason to panic. This is good news.

I would start by considering whether you have a gut instinct in favour of one choice or another. Does one option just feel right? In that case, go with your gut instinct. Psychologists tell us that instinctive decisions can be the best ones. Just go for what feels right.

If all else is equal to you personally, does someone around you care about the decision and prefer one of the options over the other? If so, go with what they want. If you don't mind if your new car is blue or green, let your partner decide!

If you (or your partner/friend/colleague) don't have a particular feeling, and all is truly equal between your options, then just pick one. If you can't, then write the options on bits of paper and pick one from a hat.

You feel unhappy

What if you have used your decision-making model and have a decision, but in the end you still feel something is not right? The decision does not feel completely comfortable. This is a trickier situation.

First, go back through your decision-making model. Have you listed all the relevant factors? Have you given them due weight? Have you correctly balanced them?

Second, can you be precise about why you feel uneasy? Is it a particular issue you need to think about a bit more? Is your subconscious indicating you have left an area unconsidered? Is what you are proposing to do morally wrong? If you can pin-point the source of your unease you can then feed it into the equation. Does it relate to one of the 'cons'? If so, it may be you need to recall the 'pros'. Face up to the fact that the decision does have its downside, but emphasise all the good things that will happen; or all the worse things that will flow from the other options. There just might not be a perfect solution.

This can be particularly relevant if the decision is going to hurt someone we are close to. We instinctively react against doing that, but it may be that the alternatives will hurt that person even more. Or the alternatives will distress another person even more. It may be that although hurt will be caused, in the long run there will be greater good. Your feeling of unease is proper, but in the broader picture the decision is the correct one.

Third, it may be you cannot be precise about what is making you uneasy. People will respond differently. My advice would be this: take a little time. There is wisdom in sleeping on a decision, but set yourself a deadline. For example, 'I will sleep on this and confirm my decision by 10 a.m. 'Or, I will go for a long walk and get some fresh air. When I come back to the office I will make the decision.' Giving yourself space away from the decision might help you understand why you feel uneasy about it. It also helps to talk to someone you trust if you are feeling uneasy. Voicing doubts makes situations clearer in our own mind.

"There is wisdom in sleeping on a decision, but set yourself a deadline."

You should trust your decision-making techniques, but instinct should not be ignored. If there is an alternative which is very close to the 'best option' that you feel uneasy about, then go for the alternative. You may not be being entirely rational, but our gut instincts can reveal some important truths that are beyond rationality. If, however, no other options are close to the 'best one' under the model, stick with it.

You want to wait

You have made the decision using a model in Chapter 3 but feel you do not have all the information you need or you believe that new information may come to light. Should you wait? Beware! It is very easy to delay implementing a decision because you do not know all the facts or you think things might change. I have written before of the human tendency many of us have to put off making a decision. Is this what you are doing? Or is there a really good reason for why there should be a delay?

Remember you are never going to know all the information. Tomorrow may bring new factors, but so might the day after and the day after that. If you wait until you know everything there is to know you will be waiting a very long time. It is easy to imagine that new bits of information might arise, but there is little point in placing weight on such vague possibilities unless you know for sure that new information will be found that will be highly significant to your decision. If you are waiting for medical test results, then that is a fact worth waiting for before you book a holiday. It's a sure piece of information that is coming and is not currently available. But if you are waiting to see if the weather in the UK improves, that is not a good reason to delay and you might as well make the decision.

Remember too that not deciding now is a decision not to act. You may miss out on this opportunity. Unless you are sure there is important new information which you will have in the very near future I would be wary of holding off making a decision just because 'new facts *might* arise'.

Once again: DECIDE!

Sometimes you just have to make yourself decide. Fix a definite time by which you will have made the decision. Ideally, tell others that by that time you have made a decision. If you feel really paralysed in decision making, ask someone else to help you. The best thing to do in that case is to offer the person the two alternatives: 'I just cannot decide between A and B. Can you decide for me?' It can be that if another person then decides A for you, you become completely convinced all of a sudden that B is what you wanted all along. Discussing decisions with others can make up our minds more firmly!

Summary

Don't let indecision mean that events make the decision for you. In this chapter we have looked at some of the reasons why people find it difficult to take that final jump in making the decision. They are often good reasons to be wary, but they are not good reasons for not making a decision. Now is the time to decide and move on. Go on, do it.

Chapter

Acting on the decision

Congratulations! You have now made the decision. You can have confidence that you have made a sensible decision based on all the available evidence. You now need to put that decision into practice. Don't delay – but be careful while you are putting the plan into action.

Acting on the decision may seem to be the easy bit, but often it is not. We will now look at the tricky issue of how to implement your decision. Timing and style of putting the decision into practice can be important. This chapter will also address those who feel paralysed – having made the decision they discover they are unable to act on it.

Explaining your decision

Depending on the context of your decision you may now need to explain your decision to others. Of course, if it is simply a personal matter that's only important to you, you won't need to explain and you can skip this section.

You might find it helpful to read my book, *How to Argue*, which provides lots of advice on how to present an argument, but here are some key points for now.

● Be clear. If you are announcing your decision make it quite clear what you have decided. This is especially important if you are importing bad news. You do not need to be heartless or blunt, but you do need to convey exactly what you mean. Avoid beating about the bush or surrounding what you are saying with obscuration. It will simply annoy your audience, suggest you are insincere or unsure and lead them to question the appropriateness of your decision.

- Think carefully about what arguments the person you are talking to will find most persuasive. It may have been that there was a range of considerations that led to your decision. They may all be good reasons, but which will be the ones that will appeal to the person you are talking to? Pitch the explanation of the decision (or 'sell', if you like) to the particular individual or target audience – your explanation of the decision to the finance director is unlikely to be the same as the one to the cleaning staff.

- How is the person you are informing of the decision likely to react? What is the impact going to be for them? What can you say to reassure them? Or to lessen any negative impact of the decision? Be sensitive to the fact that they may respond to the decision emotionally, in which case a rational explanation of the decision may not be the best response.

Where the decision reached is one that is going to directly affect someone else, it is only decent to inform them face-to-face and explain it to them. Of course, this can lead to embarrassment and confrontation, but in the long run both of you will feel better about what has happened if the decision is communicated clearly and well.

The press is full of stories of people who allegedly have chosen the wrong time or wrong place to end a relationship. It's said that the first time actress Minnie Driver found out that her relationship with actor Matt Damon was over was when he announced it on Oprah Winfrey's chat show. Earl Spencer is said to have asked for a divorce from his wife when she was relaxing in the bath. As fans of *Sex and the City* will recall, Carrie was dumped by one boyfriend through a Post-it note. And I certainly hope the American company The Break Up Bear, which delivers a teary-eyed bear with a message ending the relationship, goes out of business soon.

If you need to communicate a decision which will be distressing to another person, find a place where you can be private and have time to discuss the issue. Be completely clear about what the decision is. Don't try to disguise it. If you have decided to end a relationship then make that clear. Talking about spending slightly less time together sounds false and evasive, unless you really mean that.

Try to think in advance what the impact will be on the other person. What can you do to lessen the blow, if anything? Ideally, have some suggestions planned before you begin. If you are ending their job, do you know of other opportunities that may be available to them? Help them to move on from the impact of the decision you have made. Of course, it may be that they need time to digest the disappointing news, before they can look forward. Be sensitive to their reaction. They may want to leave the room as soon as possible.

It can be important to express how you feel sometimes. 'I am really sorry to let you down, but I had to decide which project to support – I'm not able to support both.' Give the context of the decision. 'I am afraid another company came in with a bid which was significantly lower than yours and at the end of the day we would be making much less profit if we went with you.' You can be honest without being brutal.

Action planning

Having made the decision you now need to put it into practice. That may be straightforward – you must send the e-mail or buy the new suit. But if the decision has been over a vaguer issue, it may not be so straightforward. You have made the decision, but how do you implement it? You have decided to move house or get a new job – that might be the easy bit, but what now?

There are plenty of people who have made wise decisions to do something, but then have never quite got around to implementing them. It's not good making the decision and then thinking it will automatically happen – you must make an action plan to implement it.

Here are some top tips in relation to action planning:

- Be clear where you are now. You cannot know how to move towards your goal unless you know where you are. You should have determined that before you made your decision but it is worth reminding yourself.

"You cannot know how to move towards your goal unless you know where you are."

- Be clear about your objectives. You should have done this while making your decision. Where do you want to be? Which aspect of that is negotiable and which is an absolute requirement? Never lose sight of your essential requirements; your job is to implement your decision in a way that achieves your goals. If you miss them, something has gone badly wrong. What are the key objectives, and which are desirable but not essential?

- Are your objectives achievable and measurable? There is no point in seeking to reach a goal you never can reach or one that cannot be measured. You might decide to lose five kilos in a week, but that just isn't going to happen. Your objective must be realistic. If you select too vague a goal you cannot create an action plan because you don't know where you are trying to get to.

- How are you going to get to the goal you want to reach? That may be a straightforward question and the answer obvious, but it also may not be. In which case you may need to break your plan down into smaller steps. What can you currently do that will take you closer to your goal? When I decided as a youngster that I wanted to be a lawyer, I did not know at that stage what kind of law I wanted to practise; or precisely in which capacity; let alone where or with which firm. So a big decision like that needed to be broken down into realistic smaller goals. In my case the first stage was to undertake a law degree. Without a legal qualification I would never achieve my ultimate goal. Whatever the decision you need to make, what is crucial is that you should ensure that you are always moving towards your goal. Do not be side-tracked by temporary difficulties or tempting offers which might have some short-term appeal.

- Set yourself a timetable. When can you reasonably expect to have achieved your goals? Have time limits. Be realistic. People tend to underestimate how long it will take to do a job. Build in some time for unexpected events.

- Review how you are doing. Having gone to the length of writing an action plan, it will be no good if you do not review it. You need to keep checking how you are doing. Have you missed a deadline? What could you have done better? Do you need to rewrite the action plan in light of the current situation? Have new opportunities opened up so that you can achieve your goals even more quickly?

- If you can, tell a friend or colleague about your plan. Take encouragement from them as you progress along the way. Discuss things with them when you have fallen behind. With a supporter at your side who knows what you are seeking to achieve, the journey may be easier. Studies of those dieting and trying to quit smoking suggest that having friends who can say 'well done' when you achieve your goals and urge you on when the going gets tough is very helpful. These people are far more likely to succeed than people who do not have a supportive network of friends.

- Prepare a contingency plan. If you can foresee problems, what will you do in those scenarios? Are there alternative ways to reach your goal if something goes wrong? You won't be able to cover every contingency, but it will be easier for you to face any disappointment if you already know what you will do. It is always hard to receive a set-back to your plans, but if you have already thought through how you will respond it is unlikely to look so bad.

- Foresee your weaknesses. What part of the plan are you dreading? What can you think about now to help you deal with that? It is easier to think about possible weaknesses now than when a panic sets in! Will giving yourself treats when you complete sections of the plan be an incentive?

Example action plan 1

I have decided my objective is: To find a new job.

To achieve this I need to:

1. Complete the new training course.

2. Write to my father's friend Ted and ask for some work experience.

3. Discuss my CV with Barbara and ask for advice on redrafting it.

4. Completely redraft my CV.

5. Send CV and covering letter to my five top employer choices.

6. If called for interview, discuss interview techniques with Barbara.

7. Go to the interview and get the job!

Timeline

1. By 1 September.

2. By 1 November.

3. By 31 December.

4. By 31 January.

5. By 28 February.

---

6. By 14 March.

7. By 30 June.

Reward for completing first three steps: Buy a new outfit for New Year's party.

Reward for completing step five: Day at spa or other activity of my choice.

Contingency plans

Ted may not have time to offer work experience. Then I will try contacting Mary or Steve.

Barbara may not be able to help with my CV as she is busy. Then I will contact Malcolm as he is very good at that kind of thing too.

The job applications do not lead to interviews. Then I will contact the twenty next largest firms and try again.

Forseeing weaknesses

I hate writing my CV. I will set aside time from 7–8 p.m. every evening for the week ending 20 January to write it.

I get very nervous in interviews. I will ask Barbara for advice about nerves. Maybe I will take relaxation classes (ask Fi as she knows about that kind of thing).

I must not lose sight of my goals. I will show a copy of this plan to Tom and ask him to be my buddy seeing me through this.

Example action plan 2

I have decided to/my objective is: To cut £100,000 from my department's budget.

To achieve this I need to:

1. Examine carefully the current budget.

2. Cut any items which are not essential.

3. Find cheaper suppliers for essential items.

4. Reduce employment costs by sacking one member of staff.

5. Re-examine the state of the budget.

Timeline

1. By 1 March.

2. By 7 March.

3. By 14 March.

4. By 21 March.

5. By 24 March.

Reward for completing first three steps: Theatre outing.

Reward for completing step five: Weekend break.

Contingency plans

I may not find any expenses to cut. Then I will discuss this with Tom over lunch, who is an experienced manager and may have advice.

I may not find cheaper suppliers. Then I will try to put pressure on the current suppliers to cut their charges.

Forseeing weaknesses

I get on really well with my current suppliers. I need to be firm and not let personal wishes take hold. This must be about money. I may get on well with the new suppliers.

I hate the idea of dismissing someone. I will seek advice from Frieda who has done this several times. I will arrange to meet up with Frieda later that day for support.

Summary

Having read this chapter you will have learned how to explain your decision to others. Remember to look at the decision from the perspective of the person you are talking to. Explain to them as clearly as you can why you made the decision you did.

We have also learned how to implement decisions. Draw up an action plan. Foresee where you may have difficulties in putting your decision into practice and decide now how you will deal with them. Use family and friends to help guide you through to a successful implementation of your excellent decision.

Chapter

7

Reviewing the decision

It is important to review a decision once it has been made. This helps you learn from the good decisions you have made and also from any mistakes. The best way to improve your decision-making skills is by making decisions and learning from the results. But too often people don't want to take advantage of the lessons learned by history. Don't make that mistake. This chapter will provide you with clear advice on how to look back and learn. It will conclude with a list of questions to take you through a personal analysis of decisions you have made.

We are all human. We all make mistakes. In fact, some of the most hilarious instances can result from errors. I well remember as a student having done a huge load of laundry (as usual I had left it until all my clothes were dirty) and put it on the washing line before going out for a long walk. There was soon a downpour. Not only was I soaking, so was *every* bit of clothing I owned. Fortunately, I saw the funny side and found it hilarious! A good story to dine out on for the rest of the week.

But when we've made a careful decision and it does not turn out as expected, it's important to learn from our mistakes, if indeed there has been a mistake. Sometimes there hasn't been a mistake, it's just that things didn't turn out the way we hoped. But, importantly, we must move on. So this chapter has two parts. In the first we will look at how you can learn from a mistake: what can you do better next time? What went wrong? And in the second, how can you move forward, if the decision made has turned out badly?

Learning from mistakes

If you are going to learn from your mistakes you must decide what went wrong. Don't be hard on yourself; we are simply trying to find out what happened in your decision-making process and what you can do next time, if anything, to avoid it. So here are some of the things that might have gone wrong:

- You missed out a relevant fact. When considering what to do you had not realised a crucial fact. This shows the importance of making sure you know all the relevant information before you make a decision. A common mistake is to assume that because the first few facts you come across support your initial hunch that you do not need to look any further. Next time, gather all the facts you can, even if they do not support your initial view.

- You made a false prediction. When weighing up the alternatives your prediction as to future events was in error. This may not be your fault at all. You might reasonably have assumed the facts would turn out one way but something unusual happened or someone behaved in a surprising way. The unpredictable cannot be predicted! But maybe you were unduly optimistic or unduly pessimistic. It is important to know if you tend to be inordinately cautious or over ambitious. That way you can be aware of your tendencies.

- You listened to another's advice too much or too little. Looking back at what has happened, do you pay too much attention to the views of someone else? Why did you attach such importance to their views? Was it because they are a good friend? Or because they are older or younger? On the other hand, did you fail to heed what, in retrospect, was wise advice? Why did you not listen to them? Consider whether you can learn from what has happened about taking advice from others.

- You paid too little or too much attention to your moral values. Were you too morally superior and out of touch with how things work in real life? Or do you now feel riven with guilt about your decision? Might that suggest that you had failed to attach sufficient weight to whether the decision accorded with being the kind of person you want to be? Are others criticising you for your decision as immoral? If so, are they justified? It may be that their blame is misplaced because they do not understand the facts. Or is there something in what they are saying? Maybe next time you need to attach more weight to your values and being the kind of person you want to be.

- Did you make the mistake of thinking it was too late to turn back? Sometimes people or organisations have started on a course of action and by the time it is clear they have made a mistake they feel 'we have come this far we cannot go back'. It might be someone not wanting to break off an engagement as the wedding plans are well advanced; a business that has invested in a new venture and feels it cannot lose the resources ploughed into it; or someone not wanting to trade in their car because they have spent a lot of money on repairing it. The danger in this approach is that the lost costs (the time and money already spent) are given too much weight, but the loss you will suffer if you do not change your mind or the gains you are missing out on are not taken on board. You are blinded and cannot see the misery of an unhappy marriage; the profits that could be made from an alternative venture; or the extra costs the unreliable car will incur. Focusing too much on what has been invested to date is a common error. Is that what caused the mistake in your case? Remember with decision making you must look forward, not back.

"Focusing too much on what has been invested to date is a common error."

- Did you misread how someone would react? It can be difficult to foresee how people will react. If the response of others to your decision was key to its success, did you get that wrong? Try to work out how this happened. Did you make the mistake of assuming everyone was like you? Should you have asked them how they would respond? Could you have explained the decision in a different way and would that have avoided the problem?

- Were you over-confident in your own abilities? A well-known study of drivers found that 80 per cent of respondents said they were in the top 30 per cent of drivers. Clearly most of them were in error! Making an accurate assessment of our own abilities is difficult. Confidence and optimism are admirable qualities and, arguably, essential in a business context. But these need to be tempered by realism.

- Was your reasoning correct? Be aware that in personal decisions a comparison of how the decision benefits you and others can distort your reasoning. In one study of the benefits of a decision, one group of people were offered three options. They could choose whether the decision would make:

  - $7 for themselves and $7 for another person
  - $8 for themselves and nothing for another person
  - $10 for another person and nothing for themselves

  Most people chose the middle option ($8 for themselves). However, when the same group of people were offered only the first two options most people chose the first ($7 for themselves and $7 for another person). This suggests that depriving someone of $10 skews the way people think about the decision. That's not logical. Don't worry that others will gain from your decision; if it is the right decision for you, do it, even if others will be helped. OK, the new wall you plan to build will benefit your neighbour's property. So what? If anything, that is an additional argument in favour of putting the wall up. Certainly don't think that because you are giving someone a 'freebie' that means the decision is wrong.

- A common error is to place too much weight on recent events. The latest memory is in the front of your mind. Politicians are typically guilty of this error. There is a disaster or scandal of some kind and a response is immediately found to it, regardless of whether it is in fact the issue that is most in need of attention. Because it is what everyone is talking about, politicians throw money at the issue. There are plenty of examples where, in retrospect, this looks like wasted money because the scandal was a one-off. Make sure you evaluate your decision in light of the entire scenario, not just immediate events.

- Did you make the mistake of following the crowd? Solomon Asch has a famous experiment of asking people which, of a number of lines drawn, was the shortest. Among the participants were actors in disguise. They confidently pointed to the wrong answers when first asked. About a third of those involved copied the actors, even though it should have been obvious they had got it wrong. So following the crowd is a natural thing to do. Is that where you went wrong? Did you think that everyone else cannot be wrong?! If so, remember, next time you make the decision for yourself. Maybe everyone else is right, but think through the decision for yourself and don't copy others in the first instance. If you work out they are wrong, then follow the strength of your convictions.

Moving on

What if you have made a decision and now it is clear you have made a mistake? We have discussed looking back and deciding where the error was; that is all well and good, but you need to move on. Here are some key steps.

First, ascertain what your current position is. Focus on the facts. Don't think about where you were or where you hoped to be. Where are you now?

Second, where do you want to be? Is the goal you were originally seeking to achieve still possible? Is it just that you took the wrong direction? Or has your original goal now become impossible: the person you were hoping to marry has now married someone else? The house you wanted to buy has been taken off the market? Then you need to reset your goal. It is easy to become miserable at this point – that house was just perfect, you will never find one as nice. Well, you don't know until you start looking. Few things in life are truly unique. You are likely to find another house which will be different – some things will be better and some things worse than the earlier one. You will find another partner, no doubt in some ways better and in some ways worse (perhaps she doesn't make as mean a chocolate cake), than the original object of your affection.

Or has it now transpired that what you thought was your goal is not what you want? You thought you would be happy with the new job, but now you are there it is clear that you are not. You need to be careful here. Ironically, reaching a goal can create a sense of let down. When writing a book, I get caught up in it and get driven to complete it. I look forward to sending it off. Yet when I send it off it can be strangely deflating. I have reached my goal, and yet … I miss the writing of it. So be aware that reaching a goal can be a downer. That does not mean the original goal was wrong or misplaced; it may mean that it is time to set a new goal. Many people find the journey to their goals more enjoyable than the reaching of them!

"Be aware that reaching a goal can be a downer."

There is another danger here too. Grass, as it is so often said, is greener on the other side. How many people do you know who are so thrilled when they get a new job, but when you see them several months into the job they are not excited? In part this is because many people are optimistic. The new job will be fantastic. They cannot be disappointed. So if you are deflated in reaching your goal, is it just that you had hyped up what it would be like? Or is it just the natural deflation on achieving a result? If the excitement has waned, it may not be that the goal was wrong – you decided well and journeyed well – now is the time to accept that no job is ever perfect and make the most of your new post. Or accept that the new neighbours are not what you had hoped to have, but you will still enjoy the new house.

But, of course, sometimes on reaching the goal it is clear that it was not what was hoped for. You longed to go out with Ted, but now that you are doing so, the admirable qualities seen from afar are not so apparent close up! You lusted after the new car, but now you have it, it seems rather tinny and cheap. You need to reset your goals.

In resetting your goals don't abandon everything. It is likely that there was something good about the original goal you were setting yourself. Think carefully: what is good about the goal you were first seeking; what is bad? Rethink and develop your new goal.

If you decide you have made the wrong decision, how are you going to get from where you are now to where you want to be? Go back to the decision-making tools in Chapter 3 – which option will work best in revamping your decision?

Summary

If you have made a decision which has gone wrong, ask yourself the following:

1. What went wrong with your decision making? Is there a lesson to be learnt for the next time you need to make a decision?
2. Are you still trying to reach the same goal or has your experience caused you to rethink what your goal is?
3. How can you move from where you are now to where you want to be? Don't look back and regret the past, that can't be changed; how can you learn to move forward to a better future?

Chapter

8

Putting decision making into practice

In this chapter we're going to look at some of the most common and biggest real-world decisions in a bit more detail. This is dual purpose: firstly it will give you a lot more tailored help if one of these scenarios happens to be the decision you need to make; but also it's a useful way of applying the theory to real-life situations to see how it works in practice.

Buying a house

Imagine you have decided to move house. You have visited seven houses and they all seem great. Or they all seem not quite right. But you can't make up your mind. How to decide between them? Or should you wait and see what else comes on the market? Maybe you are terrified you might make a mistake. Don't worry, by taking this logically you can confidently make a decision.

1. You must make a list of your absolute requirements. Are there conditions for your new house which are non-negotiable? These are very likely to include a maximum price! It may also be necessary that the house has a certain number of bedrooms or bathrooms. For our family it was essential there was a room big enough to fit a grand piano! You must stick strongly to your requirements. There is no point viewing a house which does not meet your absolute needs. You will get distracted and misled. Looking at a house you cannot afford is only likely to make you miserable. Focus only on those which meet your minimum requirements.

2. What are your preferable requirements? What are you looking for as desirable characteristics of a new house? Think carefully about this. What really matters? Try to come up with a list that is not too long.

3. Prepare a grid. This works well in a decision such as this. Let us imagine you are considering seven factors and seven houses. The grid may look like the one on the next page. Remember, in this example you have already determined that all the houses have your essential requirements. So when we list price they are all within your budget, but most people would like to come under budget.

	Price	Commute	Pretty	Spare room	Garden	Close to park	Environmental
House 1							
House 2							
House 3							
House 4							
House 5							
House 6							
House 7							

Mark each house out of ten for each factor:

	Price	Commute	Pretty	Spare room	Garden	Close to park	Environmental
House 1	6	3	4	2	1	2	3
House 2	5	5	3	2	2	2	2
House 3	8	6	4	8	5	3	8
House 4	2	8	7	5	5	5	6
House 5	6	7	8	6	8	7	2
House 6	4	7	5	7	9	8	9
House 7	1	8	5	7	7	7	7

The quick way of making the decision is simply to add up the scores for each house and decide which has the highest (House 6). But before moving on too quickly, consider whether all of your seven criteria are equally important. Is the closeness to the park as important as the commute? Or is prettiness more important than the spare room? Marking all the headings out of ten is not subtle enough, so you could try to give different maximums to reflect each factor's importance. For example, if the key issues for you are the price, commute and prettiness, mark these out of ten; if the spare room and garden are moderately important, mark these out of five; and if the closeness to park and environmental factors are not important, mark them out of two.

Be careful when doing this ranking, it is easy to downplay 'everyday issues'. You might think that the spare bedroom will be really useful at Christmas when your parents visit, but an extra fifteen-minute commute is not too bad. The problem with this reasoning is that fifteen minutes (each way, remember) every day will over time be a far bigger burden than the inconvenience that might arise at Christmas. Booking a nearby hotel room for a couple of nights might be a cheap price to pay for four hours less commuting a week.

Now House 5 emerges as having the highest total. In the earlier grid House 6 did particularly well on matters which were less important to you. House 6 scores the highest when all factors are equal, but House 5 scores best overall when things that matter the most are given due weight.

Having used grid-analysis, the various requirements you are looking for in your house and their relative importance have become clearer. You are now in a position to decide the particular house you wish to purchase.

	Price/10	Commute /10	Pretty/10	Spare room/5	Garden/5	Close to park/2	Environmental /2
House 1	6	3	4	1	0	0	0
House 2	5	5	3	1	1	0	0
House 3	8	6	4	4	3	0	2
House 4	2	8	7	2	3	1	1
House 5	6	7	8	3	4	1	0
House 6	4	7	5	3	4	2	2
House 7	1	8	5	3	3	1	2

Life decisions

For some people, the decisions they find themselves struggling with most are the big ones: 'I want my life to be happier, what shall I do?'; 'Things have all gone wrong, what shall I do next?'; 'I don't want to be here, where shall I go?' These are the questions that you spend ages mulling over in the wee hours, not getting very far. General dissatisfaction with life can lead to turmoil.

The reason you do not get far in figuring out how to change your life is that your worries are too vague and too big. Remember, first you need to look forward. Wondering about the past and any mistakes you have made is not going to help. The past is past and now you need to look to the future.

"Wondering about the past and any mistakes you have made is not going to help."

You need to set yourself some precise goals. Look at the following questions.

- If you could live in the shoes of one of your friends, who would you choose?
- What kind of person do you want to be?
- If a genie granted you three wishes, what would they be?
- Where would you like to be in five years' time?
- What are you doing when you are happiest?
- Looking back on your life so far, what has given you the most pride?

Answering some of these questions might give you some precise goals to reach. How can you do more of the things you enjoy doing? How can you reach one of your three wishes? Focusing on clear-cut questions such as the following will be more productive than a vague pondering on how life could get better or worse. These types of questions will help you get closer to your specific goals:

- How can I spend more time with my friends?
- How can I improve my pottery skills?
- What can I do to meet more men?

For clear answers to life's big questions you need to break down your dissatisfaction into smaller parts. Define your goals and then take small steps in trying to reach them. Decisions will become more obvious as you break down your goals into achievable stages.

Where to go on holiday

This is another kind of decision which gets people very worried. Indeed, some people get so worked up about it they need a holiday to recover from making the decision!

The first point to emphasise is that it is very unlikely you are going to make a bad mistake. Few people deeply regret their holiday choice. So you can relax. You are choosing between brilliant holidays!

Second, remember your prejudices. For some people going back to the same place again and again is ideal. Of course, it may be. What do you want from your holiday? If you want a completely stress-free time and all you want to do is lie on a beach you already know, then fair enough. Many people choose the option they know because it feels safe. But newness on holidays brings lots of interesting experiences and discoveries not had before. Often, when returning to a previous destination, the place is never quite as great as it seemed the first time.

You can probably guess what I am going to say now. You need to select what you regard as the best decision to make: do I want the familiar, or do I want the new? Once you determine your approach to the holiday, make a list using pros and cons of the individual destinations. If you decide you only want to go somewhere you've been before and you are not up for a new adventure, then list your top three holidays you've had in the past. Put down all the pros and cons for those three holidays. Use the section I wrote on pros and cons to help you. If you wish to go somewhere new, do the same thing. List your top destinations, and then the pros and cons of each. After weighing up the factors, you should have your decision made!

Who to pick for the job

Most job adverts have a list of criteria: those that are essential requirements and those that are desirable. When you choose someone for the job, these criteria should form the basis of your decision making. Following a job interview it is always tempting to make decisions about who to employ based on factors which should not be relevant: you didn't like one candidate's socks; you did like the other candidate's smile! Interviews are nearly always an artificial situation. Only rarely does an interview give a deeply revealing insight into a candidate's personality. Sitting down carefully in advance (before having met any applicants or read any letters of application) and determining what you really need from the new employee is an essential part of making a good decision when hiring a new member of staff.

So make a list of your essential requirements. If any candidate does not meet these they should not be called for an interview, or if they have been they should be removed from the list. Do not be tempted to keep them in play unless there are truly exceptional circumstances.

When thinking about the kind of person you are looking for don't restrict your essentials list to formal qualifications. It may be that aspects of a candidate's character will be important too. Do you need someone who is not only qualified but also has determination or drive? Is getting on with people an important requirement, or does that not actually matter for this job? Think carefully about how you will assess these characteristics.

Looking at the essential factors, mark each candidate out of 10 on how well they meet these. Remember, although each candidate may have met the minimum essential requirements, each will have met them to a larger or lesser degree. If one candidate is clearly better than the others on the essential requirements then you should appoint them. Do not be distracted by the other, less significant, factors.

If there is little to choose between the candidates on the most significant factors then consider the desirable requirements. Again, keep focused on the ones in the job description. Be wary if, having met the candidates, you are seeking to add new requirements to the job description. It may be there genuinely has been an error in the original description for the job. However, it is just as likely you are letting personal prejudice tilt the balance in favour of a candidate that you liked.

If character and personality are important (either as essential or desirable qualities), you will want to think about how to assess these. A formal interview is unlikely to reveal what the candidates are really like. Arranging a meeting in a less structured setting may be useful. For one job I applied for as a trainee solicitor early in my career, a group of candidates were taken on a tour of the office for forty-five minutes and at the end were told that was all. The tour was the interview, although none of us had realised it until it was too late!

Deciding whether to end a relationship

Perhaps one of the hardest decisions to make is whether to end a relationship. This is such a personal matter it is difficult to set down definite rules. However, I would suggest the one, following, absolute rule:

> You should not be in a relationship where you are suffering physical abuse or repeated verbal or mental abuse from your partner.

> Relationships characterised by abuse or attempts to control are always harmful. You deserve much better for yourself. Leave now.

Other cases where the decision needs to be made as to whether to end a relationship are less straightforward.

1. Don't rush into the decision. Most relationships go through ups and downs, disagreements are common, relying on your immediate feelings may be something you will regret. Give yourself and the relationship time. Don't properly consider leaving the relationship unless you have been feeling for some time that it is not working out.

2. Try to assess your relationship over the length of it. On a scale from one to ten where would you rate it? Your decision will be fairly easy if you are scoring 9 or 10: lucky you! If it is 5 or under this is pretty grim. Unless you can see a clear and realistic way of pushing the relationship forward, then perhaps it is time for it to end. You should expect the central relationship of your life to be doing better than this. The most difficult scenario is where you have rated the relationship at 6 to 8: it's OK but not great, or, in the title of Mire Kirshenbaum's book, *Too Good to Leave, Too Bad to Stay*. I will assume that you are in that kind of position for the following step.

3. List the things that are good about your relationship and the things that are not. If you find that difficult, consider the times when you are happy with your relationships and those when you are not. Produce a list, perhaps like this:

GOOD	BAD
Cuddles in the morning	Sharing of housework
Meals together	Lots of rows
Like the same TV shows	P spends too much time with friends
Makes me laugh	Often at work late
Sex	Doesn't want children yet
Playing Scrabble together!	Doesn't show affection often

Don't simply add up the goods and bads and make your decision. You need to think more carefully about the issues than that.

Consider how you can make the relationship work better: what can you do to increase the number or frequency of the good things? Make time to do those things that you do well as a couple. Are there similar things you could start doing that you could add to the 'good' list? If you like having meals out together, but that gets expensive, what about having picnics together? Or going out for breakfast?

Tackle the negative things too. It may be that your partner does not realise these are problems for you. He or she may think that you don't mind them staying late at work because it gives you some time to yourself. You need to discuss that. It may be that they say they don't want children yet but they have not really seriously considered the issue. If you are having rows frequently, why not read my book, *How to Argue*, to learn how to disagree in a more productive way and reduce the number of rows, or at least make them less antagonistic.

Be realistic about the cons. Maybe they are temporary: the current project at work is keeping your partner at work late, but it is not normally like that. On the other hand, some characteristics may never change. If he's naturally untidy, you are not going to change that substantially. Maybe you can persuade him to be more tidy in a few precise ways, but be realistic. If the worst issues are dealt with, is there still a problem? Is there a way for counselling to work?

4. Having thought through the pros and cons, try to come to a view about the nature of your relationship. Here are some helpful questions to ask yourself:

- Are the problems irreversible and serious?
- Are the problems just occasional or common?
- Are you working towards mutual goals or are you and your partner moving in different directions? If the latter

is the case, are these paths that can again converge or are they heading off in very different directions?

- Imagine your relationship in five years' time: will you be where you want to be? Will you be happier?
- Do you like each other; are you friends?
- Does your partner respect you?
- Do you respect your partner?
- What do your long-time friends think of your partner?
- Do you have fun together?
- Does your partner bring out your best traits? Or your worst ones?
- Would you actually be happier if you left? Or do you have so much shared history that life alone would be very empty?

Answering these questions should reveal to you the truth about what it is best to do. It may be that to answer and think through these questions you need a short break away on your own. Arrange to visit a friend who will give you time to reflect or even talk through things with you.

5. When considering ending a relationship, think about the alternatives. Some people love being single, others find it very tough. Often if people are unhappy the roots of that unhappiness lie in themselves. Are you blaming your partner for things about yourself you are unhappy with?

"Often if people are unhappy the roots of that unhappiness lie in themselves."

On the other hand, do not stay in a relationship simply because the alternative looks awful. Little is worse than a genuinely unhappy relationship. Your friends will support and help you. There may be short-term sadness and financial and practical problems, but in the grander scheme of things these will be prices worth paying. Having said this, if there are children in the relationship the decision becomes much more complicated. It is not just your happiness at stake, but theirs as well. If you are genuinely unhappy, then it could be that your state of mind is affecting how well you parent your children. But if you are just mildly unhappy and still able to get on with most things and have some fun in life, then maybe balancing your children's needs with your own is a better approach. However, be aware that children who grow up where parents fight a lot, or where verbal and emotional abuse is taking place, will themselves develop their own set of problems.

If you have children and decide to end your relationship with your partner, you then have to decide who has custody of the children. Your relationship with your ex will still remain in some respect as you are both parents of your children, so you really need to think through all the ramifications of ending your relationship if you have a family. But I will emphasise here the point that I made at the start of this section: if you are in any danger personally through physical, mental or emotional abuse, then you have no choice but to leave.

6. Be realistic. No one is perfect. It is easy to look around and see other people that you can imagine being with; to see someone that may even look a much better prospect than your current partner. But so often people who seem charming and fun are very different once you get to know them more deeply. If you expect perfection then you will always be disappointed with your partner. They are human. They are going to make mistakes, be irritable, forgetful; just like you!

Spending money

Sometimes it is everyday decisions that can cause the greatest difficulty. Many people find making decisions in shops ('Shall I buy those jeans?') the hardest. We all spend money every day, but beware of four major distractions on everyday purchases.

One is the danger of the sale. Most people are drawn to bargains; they see the jeans are £30 off: reduced from £70 to £40. They feel they are somehow going to be £30 pounds better off if they buy the jeans. Of course they are not – only if they had bought the jeans for £70 would they be better off by buying them on sale. It is well known that many stores use apparent price reductions to lure customers into purchases. Ask yourself, if the jeans were priced at £40 would you pay that? Forget the claim that there has been a price reduction: that is an advertising gimmick and you should ignore it. Just look at the price currently demanded: are you happy to pay that? The idea of price reduction to make a product look more attractive applies in many areas of spending money and is one we need to be well aware of.

The second is the lure of the credit card. Study after study has shown that people are willing to spend much more on credit cards than they would with cash. An interesting experiment organised by two business professors in the US arranged a sealed-bid auction. Half the participants were told they could only pay with cash and the others could use credit-cards. The average credit-card bid was twice that of the cash. So beware, just because cash is not leaving your purse don't think you don't have to pay. Some people try only to use cash to pay for items because that helps them focus on the issue. At the very least try to ask yourself, would I buy this if I had cash?

The third is an assumption that a lower price means lower quality. Of course this is often true, but not always. We are strongly conditioned to assume that lower price equals lower quality. People regularly report that Coke tastes better than cheaper cola drinks when they know what they are drinking, but cannot tell the difference when blindfolded. Researchers have been able to show this by getting people to taste samples of the same bottle of wine but telling them that one is from a much more expensive bottle than the others. Nearly everyone in that test found the expensive wine tasted much better. But the researchers had lied, all the samples were the same thing! So, be careful what you are paying for. Is it the name? The packaging? Or the actual product?

The fourth is that there is a real danger when making purchases of losing sight of the big picture. When you are spending a lot of money on something you can be tricked into losing sight of the smaller costs that are added on. When you are staying in an expensive hotel and a cheese sandwich is charged at £8 that does not seem unreasonable, but you would never pay that for a cheese sandwich in another context. So beware of the extras. It is human nature to think, I am spending hundreds, what is an extra fifty? But you should look at the question in isolation. Is it a good idea to spend £50 on that?

The thing many people find difficult is knowing whether something is a good price. This is, of course, not easy. It may help to do a comparison with another situation. I could eat out with my friends for the cost of this dress. If I had to choose between eating out and the dress, which would I choose? I could buy three novels for the price of this DVD: will the DVD give me more pleasure than having three new novels to read?

Be very careful when buying. The temptation of the immediate gain is in front of us; the silky blouse is soft to the touch, but the cost of repaying the credit card is in the future. Most people have far too much personal debt. The average household debt in the UK is £8,000, excluding mortgages. Most of that is on credit cards. So if you are in any doubt, the best rule is not to buy. I bet if you reminisced you could think of foolish purchases you had made that you wish you had not. I doubt you can think of many examples of where you wish you had bought something but had failed to do so. Say no when in doubt; you're worth it.

"Say no when in doubt; you're worth it."

Where to go out to eat

Another common decision that some people struggle with is where to go out to eat. Indecision in this case can end up with you being very hungry indeed! Later we will consider how to deal with situations where there is a group of you making the decision. First, let us assume it is just you.

The first issue to address is what you are hoping to get out of the evening. Is it a really important date and you don't want anything to go wrong? Or is it a more relaxed occasion and you are just looking for somewhere fun? This is important. If you want a guarantee that you will have a pleasant meal then you will want to book a restaurant that you know is good or that you have heard from a very reliable source is good. That may restrict your choice quite a bit. If a guarantee of quality is less significant then you may be more willing to take a risk. Why not go to that Bulgarian restaurant you always pass? It may not work out well, but you will have a good laugh about it if so. And you never know, it may just be brilliant food.

The second issue is, of course, price. This is not always a straightforward matter. You can go to an expensive restaurant, just have a main course and tap water and leave with not-too-expensive a bill. But is that what you want? If you went to a cheaper restaurant and had three courses and the house wine the bill may be the same, but you would have had more to eat! Different people will answer that kind of question differently. The point is that the cost of the meal does not just depend on how expensive the main dishes are, but how many courses you have, what you drink, etc., so factor it all in.

In addition to the quality and the price, there are a host of other factors that could be relevant to your choice of restaurant. Are the restaurants within walking distance – do you want to drive (are you planning to drink?); do the restaurants have pleasant décor/settings/staff; are there healthy-eating options, etc. Again, different people will put different weight on these various factors. Your choice may also depend on whether you are looking for a quiet place for a chat or a vibrant atmosphere to liven your mood. Deciding which factors are the most important for you is a crucial part of reaching your decision.

Here are a few key tips:

- Some people keep returning to the same restaurant. That is wise if you are looking for a 'guaranteed' option on an important occasion, however, even the best restaurant can lose its sparkle after several visits in close succession. The trying of new foods and different styles is in fact part of the fun. So, if it's not crucial the restaurant has to be a guaranteed success, try somewhere new.

- Most restaurants have a menu you can look at online. That way you can consider whether there are several dishes you think you might like before you set foot in the restaurant. You can also check the price. It's well worth doing your research.

- Decide which factors are important to you. Make a list of attributes (price, location, food offered, etc.) if you need to, and rank the factors in order of preference so that you know what you are really looking for.

- Narrow your choice down to the three top restaurants, then look at which one of these ticks the most boxes when it comes to the attributes you have listed. Hopefully your choice will be obvious.

Once you have made your choice, enjoy it! You will ruin your evening if you spend your entire meal saying to your friend, 'Oh, it's nowhere as good as the place down the road'. That may be true, but there are almost inevitably some ways in which it is better. Anyway, enjoy the evening you have and get the most from it.

The issue of deciding on a restaurant can be particularly difficult if there is a group of people involved. I am sure you have been at an event where it is agreed that you will all go out for a meal and one person shouts out 'pizza'; another 'Indian'; another 'Chinese' and soon everyone is talking and it seems impossible to come up with a solution that will please everyone. In this case, I would recommend this course of action.

Imagine you are a group of five. Let everyone choose one restaurant. The first person (use alphabetical order if you cannot agree) chooses from the five nominated restaurants one restaurant that they do not like – that one is then removed from the list. The next person removes his least favourite one from the list. The third person removes another from the list. You are left with two restaurants and two people. The two of them get to choose which (together) they wish to remove, and you are left with the final choice. This way you should ensure that at least everyone is reasonably happy. You might need to modify this if someone has an allergy or special dietary requirement so that only restaurants which meet their needs are used in making the decision. Of course, most restaurants these days can cater for most dietary requirements.

Medical decisions

One of the more traumatic decisions you may need to make is about your own health. These are decisions we dread to take. Indeed, perhaps we should start by emphasising that if you are worried about your health you should seek medical advice. Delaying making the decision to see the doctor can have catastrophic effects. No one has died by going to see their doctor too early. Sadly, far too many people have died because they have delayed going to see their doctor.

In the old days medical paternalism ruled the day. The job of the patient was to tell the doctor their symptoms; the job of the doctor was to tell the patient what treatment was appropriate and what to do. The patient was just expected to follow orders. That has all changed. Many doctors these days see medical decisions as best made jointly between the patient and the doctor. The doctor will use his or her expertise to diagnose but typically then offer the patient a range of treatments. Together the doctor and patient will decide what is best.

First, it is crucial that you understand what is wrong with you. If the doctor cannot explain it clearly ask if there is a leaflet or a website which can give you information. It may be that you are so upset at the news you are being given that you cannot take in all the doctor is saying. Don't be at all embarrassed to ask for some written information. Indeed, many doctors will offer it. It is important you know the facts so that you can make a sound decision.

"Don't be at all embarrassed to ask for some written information."

Second, be clear as to what the options are. You doctor should explain the main ones, but may not offer all of them. Some treatments may not be available on the National Health Service or (if you have one) on your insurance policy. Doctors should be open, if you ask them, about other treatments which are not offered, but might be available.

Third, and this is the bit which people find hardest, be clear as to the risks attached to each treatment. There are four crucial bits of information you need to make sure you have clear in your mind.

- What is the chance of the treatment working?
- If the treatment works, what will it achieve? Is it a cure or merely treating the symptoms?
- What is the chance of side effects?
- What is the severity of the side effects?

Fairly obviously, you want to choose the treatment which has the best chance of giving you a full recovery but with the least serious side effects. However, people find it difficult to think through their options. What you need to do is this: first, list a score out of 100 for each treatment that is being offered. 100 represents a complete recovery; 0 is no change at all. You are listing the value the treatment will be to you. Second, consider the chance the treatment will succeed. This is normally a per cent (e.g. 50 per cent chance of success). You then need to multiply the value of the treatment by the chance of success. So, if you rated the treatment's effect, if successful, at 80, but it only has a 50 per cent chance of success, that gives it an overall figure of 40. You can use a calculator or ask a friend if your maths is not up to it!

The important point to notice about evaluating the benefits of various treatments is that it may be that one treatment offers a small chance of a complete recovery and another offers a high chance of partial recovery.

	Value of treatment		Chance of success	Total
Treatment A	100	×	10%	10
Treatment B	50	×	100%	50

Here, treatment B, although offering only a partial success, is a better choice because it is most likely to produce the good outcome.

But just looking at the benefits is not enough; you must also consider the side effects. You need to look at the total side effects and decide how bad they are: from 100 for dying down to 0 for no negative impact at all. Remember that the doctor (or a website) can list all of the possible negative impacts, but these might not be negative impacts for you. If the medication has the effect of making your eyebrows fall out, for some people that would be a serious matter, for others it might count for very little. Doctors are required to mention the factors a reasonable patient might consider. There is no reason for you to attach weight to them if, for you, they are insignificant. As with the benefits one, you need to multiply the assessment out of one hundred by the percentage likelihood that they will arise.

	Value to me	Likelihood	Total risk
Treatment A:			
Impotence	50	20%	10
Eyebrows fall out	10	50%	5
Treatment B:			
Stiffness in joints	50	2%	1
Heart attack	100	1%	1

At first these results seem surprising. They suggest the risks of treatment A are worse than for treatment B. But that is right. Although the consequences of treatment B are more serious, they are very unlikely to arise. Risks of 1 to 2 per cent only occur one or two in a hundred times. Most patients when making decisions are so terrified by the terrible-sounding harmful side effects that they forget to take into account the likelihood of them happening.

In our case, treatment B is the better option: it is most likely to produce the most positive impact and there is a low chance of the negative side effects.

If all of these figures are too complex, remember the simple issue you are looking for: what is the most likely effect of this medical treatment? Treatment A with a less than 50 per cent chance of providing a cure is much more likely not to work than treatment B. Not only that, treatment A is much more likely to have a harmful effect.

Statistics can confuse and worry people. Alternatively, you could ask the doctor to put it into words: does this treatment have a very high, fairly high, low or very low risk of success? Is the risk of the side effects very high, fairly high, low or very low? While not as precise as the numbers, asking those questions will give you a good idea of what you are facing.

Deciding 'no'

Given that most people are extraordinarily busy, it is surprising that many people find it difficult to say 'no'. First, we will explore why people find it difficult to make the decision to say no and then look at why, even if they have decided to say no, they still find it hard to put that decision into practice.

So why do people find it hard to say no? If you can be aware of the reasons, then you can make sure you take these into account when making a decision.

First, many people like to help others. If someone asks for help and you say 'no', that can sound mean or selfish. Of course, it would indeed be selfish if you could help someone out a great deal with only a little effort. But consider whether that is true in your case. Are you so burdened that you cannot help on this occasion? Remember this: if you agree to help but find that you cannot do what you have been asked to do or cannot do it properly, you are probably going to cause great inconvenience. It would have been much better to say no in the first place. Is there someone else who could do the job, who might even enjoy it more than you or for whom it would be much less bother? It is not necessarily selfish to say no, in fact, it might be the most selfless thing to do.

Second, people don't like to say no because they don't want to be rude. Of course it is possible to say no in a rude way, but you can also say no in a nice way. We will see how to do this shortly.

Third, people are afraid of conflict. The person asking the favour may stop being their friend if they say no, or their friendship may be damaged. But I beg to disagree. I recently asked a colleague to do a favour for me and she appeared happily to agree. I later found out that she had already been working more than fourteen hours a day. I felt awful that I had asked her to do more. There were plenty of other people I could have asked, if I had realised how busy she had been. I certainly won't ask her to do any favours again. I am not sure her saying yes actually improved our relationship, it rather damaged it. So be honest with your friends. If you explain politely why on this occasion you cannot help out they will understand.

Fourth, a common reason for not saying no is that you are worried you will be closing a door. You are offered a few hours overtime, but if you say no on this occasion will you be offered extra hours again? You are offered a small job by a client, if you don't take it will they offer you a big job when one comes around? These are legitimate concerns, but don't give them too much weight. You can make it clear that your no on this occasion is not meaning you never want to take up opportunities. Remember too that by taking up the opportunity and not doing a good job you might in fact incur far worse consequences than turning down an opportunity.

"A common reason for not saying no is that you are worried you will be closing a door."

Even if you have decided to say no some people find that difficult to put into practice. It is wrongly assumed that saying no is something negative, but you can turn it into a positive. How you say no is of crucial importance. Here are some top tips on saying no:

1. Be clear. There is nothing more annoying than talking to someone who is trying to say 'no' while appearing to say 'yes'. For example, a person says something like: 'If you cannot find anyone else, then I would be happy to do it.' They are probably meaning they don't want to do it, but their message comes across as disingenuous or false. If you mean no, then say no.

2. If you say no explain why, in general terms: 'I cannot agree to take this on at the moment because I have too many other projects'. There is a danger in being blunt; just saying 'no' can sound unfriendly and unhelpful, so give a reason, but be careful about being too specific because otherwise the other person might try to talk you round. If you say, 'I cannot help as I have to look after my children that afternoon,' you may find the other person offering to look after your children to free you to take the job! So better just to say something like, 'I am afraid family commitments mean I cannot take you up on this offer.'

3. If you are worried about closing the door on other opportunities, try to keep the door open. 'I am afraid my diary is completely full at the moment, but why don't I phone you at the start of January and we can see if we can do business.' You are making it clear that you do want to do business with the client, even if it is not possible right at this moment.

4. When saying no try to be positive. So rather than saying, 'I am exhausted and cannot do any more work,' get across the

message you are popular and in demand. 'I have so many exciting projects going at the moment, I am having to delay taking any more on.'

5. If possible, recommend someone else. This has multiple benefits. First, it shows you are concerned about the problem the other person has and you are willing to make an effort to find someone to help. Second, the person you recommend may be thrilled that they have been recommended by you. Maybe they will return the favour one day.

6. Don't feel pressurised into saying yes. If the other person is badgering you and trying to persuade you to say yes, please don't give in. A polite way out is always to say, 'Let me think about this a little more and I will get back to you.' That will give you time to think it through. But don't change your mind just because you are under pressure.

7. It is absolutely crucial to say no if you cannot do the job. This may be because you do not have the time or because you do not have the ability. It is the worst outcome to say yes and then not complete the job. So, if you are in doubt, say no. You can be honest that you are not trained to do that work and explain what area of work your expertise is in. Everyone will appreciate your honesty and will be likely to come back with work that does fall within your area of expertise.

I hope these suggestions have helped you understand how to say no. We are all only human, and we can only do so much, so if you decide to say no, now you have the tools to go about it. Be brave, say 'no' when necessary and turn it into a positive experience.

Summary

In this chapter we have looked at some specific decisions that need making. You now know how to make decisions in everyday situations such as going on holiday, and also in bigger situations such as buying a house or choosing a course of medical treatment. You are fast becoming an expert in making decisions.

Chapter

9

Decisions involving more than one person

Like it or not, many decisions are not yours alone to take. Sometimes you will have to decide with one other person, other times as part of a group. What techniques and approaches work best in these situations?

Decisions to be made as a couple

My wife and I went to a store recently to choose a range of bits for a new kitchen. The store manager was dumbfounded when we left in under ten minutes with all the decisions made. That would take hours for many couples. My friends would say that I just let my wife make all the decisions, but that isn't true! We have just learned to make quick decisions as a couple.

Here are some tips for making decisions as a couple:

1. **Be open and honest**. Tell your partner exactly what you like; be especially clear about what your boundaries are. If you hate pink and you are making a decision about wallpaper, say so. If what you really care about is that the wallpaper has flowers on it, make that point. It is remarkable that when voicing clearly our crucial desires the decision becomes obvious: orange flowers it must be! Many couples find it difficult to make decisions because they try to be 'nice' and are not honest. You can make it clear what your views are without being rude. Remember, when making a decision there is no need for personal abuse. Set down what you are wanting and why. Do not expect your partner to read your mind!

2. **Listen**. A decision made by a couple is only going to work well if it is a decision which both parties are happy with. You must listen carefully to the views of your partner and ensure the decision, at the very least, goes some way towards meeting their desires. In some couples, one party may be naturally more diffident and reluctant to state their will. If that is you, then doing so can be unfair on your partner. If they love you they will want to take your wishes into account, so speak up! If the quiet one is your partner, give them time and encouragement to express what they want. There is nothing worse in a relationship than one party keeping quiet during the decision making, only for the other party to find out once the decision has been made that they disagree.

3. **Compromise**. Remember there are two ways you can compromise: one is to seek to make the decision which reflects the views of both parties; the other is to agree one person makes one decision and the other person another. For example, one partner chooses the wallpaper and the other chooses the curtains. Of course you want to avoid the situation where neither person gets exactly what they want and both are unhappy. Using the first method of compromise, where the decision reflects both parties' wishes, perhaps choose two options for the wallpaper, both of which you yourself like, and let your partner choose the one they prefer of those two options. This approach of choosing two options that you are happy with and then allowing your partner to make the final decision (or vice versa) is an amicable way to compromise and reach a decision that can be used in many contexts.

4. **Don't argue for the sake of it**. If your partner chooses the cutlery she absolutely loves and you are OK with it, then let her have it. It's not what you would have chosen, but it is probably not worth making a point about it. There is no use seeking to get your way on everything – that is not likely to lead to a happy relationship.

5. **Keep things in perspective**. Your relationship is more important than most decisions. Don't let disagreements get between you. If the decision-making process is getting too intense, have some fun times together. There are nearly always more things that hold you together than keep you apart.

"Your relationship is more important than most decisions."

6. **Keep mutual responsibility for decisions**. Some people enjoy letting their partner make the decisions and then blaming them for decisions when they go wrong. That is unfair. Making decisions should be shared and responsibility should be shared. If you make a decision and it is the wrong one, do not try to blame the other party. A relationship should not be about winning or losing, proving the other person right or wrong, but working together for the good of you both.

7. **Choose together to delegate certain decisions, if appropriate**. I am rubbish with cars; my wife makes all the decisions regarding the day-to-day upkeep of the car and we have both agreed that car decisions are her remit. Delegating certain types of decision can save time as long as both parties agree to delegate these decisions. Put conditions on the delegation, e.g. if the car repair is more than £200, can we discuss it first?

Finally, remember that even in the most perfect relationships couples don't always agree! Most relationships flourish on differences of style, opinion and approach. Relish that and realise you won't always see things from the same perspective, but that is part of why your relationship works. It is a matter of finding out how you can mesh your differences and weave together two ways of thinking. Certainly don't think your relationship is not going well because you cannot agree on small things – it is probably a sign of strength, not weakness, that you are being open with each other.

Decisions in a group

Much of this book has assumed you are taking a decision on your own. The issues are somewhat different when you are making decisions with one other person, and more complex as part of a group. Here are some key principles:

1. A group will make better decisions where there is trust and mutual communication. Relationships break down when one person assumes the worst in another. If someone thinks other group members' decisions are based on bad motives or that their arguments are insincere, it's impossible to make good decisions. Sound decisions rely on there being trust and an acknowledgement that whatever disagreements might arise there is acceptance that people are trying to do the best for the group. This means it is crucial to spend time establishing community and good relationships. If there are bad relationships between members it is essential there is reconciliation or else the group cannot operate as a successful decision maker. It is important that everyone in the group feels they have a voice and are listened to. The entire group needs to 'own' whatever decision is made. So a dominant personality who tells everyone else what to do is not helpful.

"It is important that everyone in the group feels they have a voice and are listened to."

2. The group needs to be persuaded that there is a problem that needs addressing. If individuals tend to be conservative then groups are even more so. In part this is because if one person seems reluctant to change then the group naturally feels reluctant to challenge their view. The group needs to think about what its goals are, what characteristics it wants, and whether it is achieving its goals to the best of its abilities. If its purpose is to make money: is it making money? Could it

make more money? If the group is designed to help disabled people, is it doing that and could it do it better? If the group sees itself as outward looking, is it doing that as best it can? Drawing on the ethos and goals of the group is an important way of demonstrating that there is a problem which needs addressing. It is important that the entire group recognises there is a problem. If you try to push ahead an agenda for change when many in the group are not persuaded that 'something must be done', you are going to struggle to succeed. So before a decision can be made, first figure out exactly what the problem is which is being addressed.

3. Having established that there is a problem, you need to ensure there is agreement on what your specific goals are. Simply identifying a problem without identifying an end point is no good. The group is losing members. That may be a problem, but there is no way to address it until you determine where you want to be. Do you want to find new members or get the old ones back? Are there things you are not doing that you should be? If the group is not making as much money as it used to, what is your target?

4. Weigh up the options; having identified the goal, consider the ways in which the group might reach it. The kinds of decision making mentioned in Chapter 3 can be used here. Encourage members of the group to look at the benefits and disadvantages various factors make to themselves personally. If necessary, remind everyone what kind of group they are trying to be and what the objectives of the group are.

If you are leading the group you need to think carefully about the different members who will be involved in making the decision. What will help them buy into a decision? What will be motivating them? When you present the alternatives, try to make sure that the perceptions of all the relevant people are included.

After using a decision-making model such as a tree diagram or grid analysis, take a vote. If there is clear consensus, then the decision has been made. But if there is not, take a step back and listen to why people are not in agreement. Work through the thorny issues and try to find the central issues of concern. Give the individual factors specific weight, and use your model once again. You could also try a different decision-making model to see if that helps. It is important that there is a clear majority when taking a group decision, so keep working at it until you get an agreeable solution.

5. When implementing the decision, give as many people in the group as possible a role to play. Not only should people feel a part of the decision making, they should also feel part of the solution. Ownership of the decision and its implementation will build cohesiveness in the group and strengthen future decision-making ventures.

6. You may need to seek a compromise. Sometimes group decisions cannot have a solution which pleases everyone. For example, the extended family is getting together for a reunion; half want to go to the beach and the other half wish to have a quiet country retreat. How to make everyone happy? You can still take a group decision by defining the over-arching goals to the decision: perhaps to see relatives you haven't seen for years, in which case where you meet up doesn't matter; perhaps to make it very accessible for young families; perhaps to find the most central location. Get everyone to agree which issue is the most important, and base your decision on this. By listing the most important factors, and getting people to agree these are the most important issues, you can sideline less important issues, such as who will organise the meal rota.

Dangers in group decision making

There are dangers of decisions being made in groups and you need to be aware of these so that you can try to avoid them.

- **The decision-making process loses its focus**. With many people making different points, and maybe with different agendas, the discussion seems not to move forward. This is a common problem. It is important that early on the goals of the group are identified and the current position is established. Then the central question of how to move from here to there can be addressed, with attention focused on that.

- **One person seeks to dominate**. Sometimes there is a danger that a single dominant individual seeks to get their way in the decision. It is very important that in such a case the person chairing the group, or other members, make sure everyone gets heard. People should not feel intimidated into not expressing their views – that will often lead to wrong decisions being made. The best decisions will hear a range of perspectives and approaches; just considering one will weaken the quality of the decision. If necessary, suggest that you go round the table with each person expressing their views. Similarly, if you are finding you are talking too much, encourage other people to speak up.

- **Try to be a peace maker**. If the group is dividing, try to find a middle path. What issues are there agreement on and where is there no consensus? Keep the focus on the common points. If there are 'difficult' individuals, seek to find a way for them to feel they have 'won' something, even if the decision is not going their way. For some people, the actual result matters less than the feeling they have 'won'; sometimes making a big deal of giving them a token trophy means they are less concerned about other issues.

- **Allowing people time to think about an issue before a meeting is always wise**. Send around a memo before the meeting, setting out the issues that will be discussed, or announce in advance the key issues to be addressed. Otherwise, there is a danger of people just talking 'off the top of their heads' in a meeting.

Summary

Making decisions with someone else or in a group can be a rewarding experience. It can strengthen relationships as you begin to understand everyone better and see issues from someone else's point of view. Make sure everyone has the chance to have their say; so listen, communicate, compromise and keep focused on your joint goals. That way you will be able to make great decisions together.

Chapter

10

Making decisions fast

Sometimes you need to respond quickly. You have been asked out; a business proposition has been put to you; an emergency has arisen and you need to do something. This chapter seeks to provide you with help in making an 'on the spot' decision.

First, make sure you really do need to make the decision fast. In many cases, explaining that you would like to think about the issue is perfectly reasonable. Don't feel under pressure to make a decision you feel unsure about unless you absolutely have to. Don't let people coerce you into a decision (that is what bad door-to-door sales people do); it is reasonable to let a person take time over a decision when possible. If you feel coerced it is probably best not to make a decision, or just say no.

Let us assume, however, that you *do* have to make that quick decision. Here are some key principles to help you make the right decision:

1. Follow your gut instinct. Psychologists tell us that people's instinctive reaction is often the right one. Indeed, spending a long time thinking about something and discussing it with others can lead to a worse decision than following your instincts. So, if your gut is telling you what to do, then do it.

2. Go back to the list of characteristics that we saw in Chapter 2. Which characteristic are you most seeking to emulate? If you are trying to be a loving person then ask: what would a loving person do? If a driven person what would a driven person do? Or if you know someone you particularly admire: what would they do in this situation?

3. Consult. If there is time call a dependable friend or a colleague. The difficulty with a rushed decision is that it is easy to overlook a crucial angle or potential consequence.

Quickly getting the views of someone else is likely to help avoid that.

4. Delegate. If you feel you just cannot make the choice then find a trusted friend or colleague and ask them to decide.

5. Can you make a temporary decision to give you more time to think through what to do? A key employee who is heading up an important project suddenly resigns; can you appoint a temporary replacement? You will need time to think through how, if at all, your employee is to be replaced. Put in the temporary placement immediately and give yourself time to respond to the full situation later. Many emergencies can be dealt with in this way; you don't want to make a rushed permanent decision which will have long-term consequences.

6. Focus on the key question. This will depend on the context. In a business it might be: what will make us most money? Or in a personal decision: what are my goals? Is this really me? There may not be time to think through all the issues but you won't be going far wrong if you are making money in your business or you are following your dreams.

7. If all else fails, toss a coin. But hold on – there's more to my suggestion than that. Choose, say, heads for yes and tails for no. Toss the coin and see how it lands. What is your

response? Do you feel pleased? Or disappointed? I remember doing this and feeling disappointed with the result. I decided to make it the best of three, and then five, until I got the answer I wanted! It would have been more sensible to just use the first flip and realise that my unhappiness at the heads told me the correct answer to my decision.

Avoiding a rushed decision

It is normally best to work through solutions to emergencies in advance. If there is a fire in a building, a clear evacuation plan which already exists and has been publicised is likely to work better than everyone responding to the situation in a panic.

Try to predict situations in advance so that you know in general what to do. In a business, work through your contingency plans. Some difficulties are more predictable: you lose a member of staff; a supplier fails to deliver; your computer system breaks down; a creditor doesn't pay. For such events have in place a set response which has been thought through and prepared for.

In home life, think through scenarios where you might feel over-whelmed and need to make a decision but can't think straight. Who will get the children if you are stuck in traffic? What will happen if you are suddenly ill? Have a contingency plan for rea-sonably likely scenarios and as a result you might find yourself stocking up the freezer a bit better, or having a handy compre-hensive list of local tradesmen, taxi numbers, mobile numbers for neighbours and colleagues. We can make our day-to-day life decisions a lot easier if we plan a little in advance for many pos-sible eventualities.

"Think through scenarios where you might feel overwhelmed and need to make a decision but can't think straight."

Summary

In this chapter you have learned how to make decisions quickly. Sometimes there isn't time to go through the full decision-making process, in which case try to follow your gut instinct; delegate the decision or quickly consult with a trusted friend; or focus on the key question. If all else fails, toss a coin and consider your response to the outcome. If you are not disappointed, follow the decision of the coin.

Chapter

11

Practise decision making

In this chapter you can have a go at practising decision making. Fortunately for this exercise it does not matter what you decide. These are just for fun. But hopefully the next few pages will give you confidence that you can use the lessons learned in this book for real-life decisions.

Bob and Jim

Can you help Bob and Jim? They have set up home together and have decided to buy a new car. However, they have almost immediately reached an impasse. Bob has always longed for a fast, red sports car. For him, looks are everything and he wants a car which will fulfil his dreams. Jim is less idealistic; he wants a car which is safe and does good mileage. Fortunately they both agree that £10,000 is the maximum they can afford to pay. You might think they are not well suited, but often opposites attract. How would you go about advising them to reach a decision together?

It's important to realise that Bob and Jim have already agreed on quite a bit. They may be relieved to see that their end goals are not completely opposite – they have both agreed that they need to buy a new car and they have agreed on a price. So although there are other differences, we can reassure them that they have done pretty well so far. But how to move forward? What would you suggest?

I would recommend they list the different criteria that they each consider to be important in a car. What would they put? From the information we have been given that would appear to be the following:

- Sport model
- Safety
- Speed
- Red
- Economy/mileage

Now we can ask Bob and Jim to give a value from 0 to 10 for the importance they each attach to these various criteria:

	BOB	JIM
Trendy look	10	4
Safety	9	10
Speed	4	2
Red	3	0
Economy	8	9

This is interesting because it shows that when they have actually come down to isolate the criteria the picture is not the same as might be thought. Although Bob mentioned he really wanted a red car, in fact on reflection he has decided that it was not the colour that was important. Also, once we separate the trendy look from the speed it is clear it is the former that is more important to Bob than the latter. The chart tells us, too, that Bob has ranked economy high, even though he did not mention that at first.

There is an important lesson here. Sometimes someone uses a generic term to describe what they want (a 'sports car'; a 'relaxing holiday') but it is necessary to break that down more specifically into what they mean. For Bob, what he really wants is a sporty appearance, rather than a speedy car. Maybe the person who says they want a relaxing holiday actually means they want some time each day to rest by the beach, rather than that they do not want to spend any energy at all!

We have got quite far with Bob and Jim now: they have both ranked economy and safety high, but ideally with a trendy look. Having agreed that much they can set off to try out some cars and if they keep focused on these three criteria they should be able to find something they will both like.

You can work through this scenario again if you wish, this time putting in your own hypothetical values into the Bob and Jim chart. Practise making the decision as if you were them. You can even try this with another person, letting them put down Jim's values while you put in Bob's. Actual practice at decision-making means we understand the tools and can use them naturally and easily when we need to. For this reason it's well worthwhile investing time with work-based teams to practise group decision making in a fictional scenario as a training exercise. The same goes for small family issues such as where to go for a day out, so that when the big issues come along you are well rehearsed!

"Practise making the decision as if you were them."

A new job offer

Imagine you were offered a new job in a different city. How would you go about making that decision?

I would suggest you would need to consider what your key goals in life are. What really matters to you? This is a rather deep question, but it is worth trying to think this through so that when big decisions come along you are prepared and will know what your values are and what your goals in life are.

Back to the new job offer: of course only you can produce a list of the important factors (and please do so now, if you wish) but here are some of the things you might care about:

- Friends
- Money
- Stress levels
- Fulfilment of the job
- Ease of commute
- Impact on family
- Where would you live?

For each of these, will your move to a different city and the new job bring you closer or further from your goals in these areas? Are your goals all equal or are some especially important?

Another way of thinking about it is to ask what you love doing now and what you would like to do but at the moment cannot?

I like:

- Jogging
- Book club
- Chatting with work colleagues over coffee
- My friendly corner shop
- Great cinema nearby.

I would like to:

- See my dad more often
- Take up French classes
- Travel more
- Meet different people
- Sleep more!

How will your move impact on the things you like doing and the things you would like to do? Will it make it harder to do the things you enjoy doing? Will it open up new opportunities to engage in activities you have not had the chance to do before?

Did you come up with issues that I didn't? Did I come up with issues you didn't? What can you learn from that?

This might be enough to have helped you with making your decision on whether to go for the new job or not, but if you are still not sure, use one of the decision-making models. For example, now that you have determined the main issues, you can use grid analysis to weigh up your different options. Your grid could look something like this:

	New job	Present job
Commute		
Friends		
Sleep		
Money		
See Dad		

Fill in the values. Add up the columns. The decision will be made, hopefully! If not, give your factors individual weight (out of 10, out of 5, out of 2, and add up the columns again). The decision should be obvious.

You discover your best friend is being unfaithful to his wife, who is also your friend, do you tell her?

This is the kind of dilemma which can be the stuff of party games. But it happens. It is the sort of decision which is especially difficult for many people. It seems that you are faced with two awful alternatives, so what do you do? You will be treating the wife badly if you do nothing; but treating the husband badly if you do tell on him. What would you do?

I would start by reassuring myself. First, this situation is not my fault; I am not the one who has behaved badly, my friend has. This situation is going to end in tears but ultimately that is not my fault. So I must not be too harsh with myself. I did not choose to get into this mess. Second, it is clear that whatever happens people are going to get hurt. There is no simple solution leading to smiles all round. That's not going to happen. Therefore whatever choice I make I must realise from the outset that it will cause pain. I must brace myself for that and make sure I do not blame myself for that. Third, there is no right answer to a dilemma of this kind. So much will depend on how the parties themselves resolve this issue and that is out of my control. A good case can be made for either being quiet or speaking. The decision won't be a bad one, whatever I do.

Where to move on from there? What factors would you use to resolve this dilemma? I would find it helpful to go back to some of the characteristics I listed in Chapter 2 and ask myself, 'What would a kind person do? What would a person committed to truth do? What would be a gentle response?' That might help me resolve the issue, depending very much on the circumstances of the case.

You might consider thinking through the consequences of telling and not telling. Ask yourself:

- What is likely to happen if I do tell?
- What is likely to happen if I do not tell?

But what to do if the answer is still not clear? Is there anything else to be done? Well, here I would consider discussing my dilemma with a friend. I would, of course, choose someone who did not know the couple and keep their identity secret to protect confidentiality. I would probably tell my friend that I do not want them to tell me what to do, but rather ask them to help me think through the issues. Most of my friends would understand exactly what I mean by that. Maybe in just describing the issues to my friend and talking about it out loud, the answer would be clear.

If all else fails I might fall back on some basic moral principles. Truth is generally better than falsehood. Relationships based on lies are not good ones. That might, depending on the circumstances, lead me to conclude I should disclose what I know to the wife.

But, and this is very important, having made that decision I must then decide how to act on it. If someone is going to tell the wife in this case: how? Think carefully about this. There are a range of ways of telling her: by letter, e-mail, face-to-face? Or is it better to give your friend the chance to tell her? 'I am going to tell your wife next week what I know unless you tell her yourself.' That might be the best option. What can you do to lessen the blow of the decision? If you know your decision is going to lead to bad consequences, can you offer support or put in place ways of protecting the person who will be harmed?

"What can you do to lessen the blow of the decision?"

Decisions such as this should not be avoided. We all have a tendency to look the other way and not get involved when faced with a difficult dilemma. But by not taking an active decision to say nothing about the infidelity, you are then not able to implement your decision by putting support measures in place for your friend who is being cheated on. Face a decision, work through the decision, decide, and then act.

Group decision making

You are a keen member of a committee in charge of a local charity that runs an after-school club for children with learning disabilities. The group is very excited because it has received a £10,000 grant, but unfortunately the members cannot agree on how to spend the grant and have fallen into three camps:

- OPTION 1: The money should be spent on paying the two employed charity workers a better wage.
- OPTION 2: The money should be spent on new equipment.
- OPTION 3: The money should be spent on setting up a weekend club for the children.

The group is in deadlock, what can be done?

The first point to make is that all three suggestions are good ones. The group is in a happy position of choosing between three good options – many voluntary groups are facing financial shortfalls and having to choose between bad options. Also, as all the options are good the group is not going to make a bad decision. It is important that everyone in the group is encouraged to view the decision in a positive light: an exciting opportunity; not a source of stress.

Remember it is important that in group decisions everyone involved understands each other. How might we do that? One suggestion I have is to arrange a listening meeting. There will be no arguments, just an opportunity for each group member to present their views to the others. The aim is to understand where each other is coming from. Just to listen. That can be a helpful exercise in itself. Generally in committees and groups people do too much talking and not enough listening.

An important point at this juncture is to try to work out what is most important for each group member. What is really important to them? Encourage the factions in the group to explain their key desire. It might appear, for example, that when it comes to specifics the key points are:

- The charity workers are under financial stress and the committee members are worried about them.
- The equipment in the room is out of date.
- Parents of the children are finding weekends difficult.

Now that the worries are clearer, compromise becomes easier. Can you see any? Maybe if the club opens at weekends we can pay the charity workers more and relieve the parents of the weekend stress. Supporters of options 1 and 3 might both be happy. Of course, that will only succeed if the workers are able to work at the weekend. Or is there another way to deal with the weekend stress? Perhaps just arranging an informal gathering in a parent's home? That might not require any of the charity's money and it can focus on the other two options. Or what about saying to the charity workers that if they are able to find free or cheap equipment then their wages can be raised? There may well be a range of alternatives of this kind to satisfy the needs of all of the members. This looks like a situation where the money can be used, along with other ways of acting, to make everyone happy, or at least fairly happy!

If this hasn't worked, how can a decision be reached? The key may be to focus the group on the goal of the charity: the well-being of the children with learning disabilities. Which of these decisions will best promote their well-being? Do the children really mind if the equipment is out of date? Are the wages of the workers affecting how well they are doing their job? Would the children be better off at weekends with their families or in the club? Asking these questions may produce a clear answer.

The final page

So now you are in a position to make excellent decisions. Here, just to remind you, are some key things to remember:

- Gather the facts.
- Think about what matters to you.
- Set your goal – what are you aiming to achieve?
- Know your tendencies.
- Get it down on paper: using a model (e.g. Pros and Cons)
- Write an action plan.
- Act!

I cannot promise that you will never make a decision that turns out wrong. That is because we never know the future. But if you follow the advice in this book you will make the best decisions you can. You can be confident your decisions are made for really good reasons and based on the best available information. Go forth … and DECIDE.

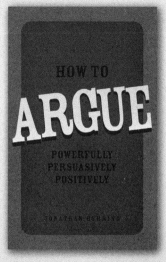

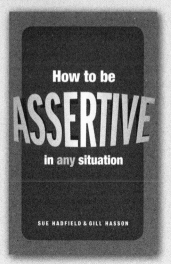